S U R P R I S E D by Suffering

RC

Surprised

SPROUL

by Suffering

TYNDALE HOUSE PUBLISHERS, INC.
Wheaton, Illinois

Scripture quotations are taken from The New King
James Version. Copyright © 1979, 1980, 1982,
Thomas Nelson Inc., Publishers.

Library of Congress Catalog Card Number 88-51836
ISBN 0-8423-6696-2 (HC)
ISBN 0-8423-6624-5 (SC)

Printed in the United States of America

00 99 98 97 96 95 94
7   6   5   4   3   2   1

For Alissa Erin Dick
stillborn infant
until we meet in heaven

PART ONE
Suffering and Death

PART TWO
Life After Death

CONTENTS

INTRODUCTION

My eyes were riveted to the clock on the waiting room wall. It was a sterile timepiece, one designed for pure utility. It had no ornamentation; it added nothing to the warmth of the room. Its sole purpose was to display the current moment in world history.

Behind closed doors people were suspended in time. For some, the minutes that were passing were the final minutes of life.

I was among those waiting. Families were gathered in a vigil for loved ones. They waited for news of the outcome of surgery. Outside, those who were healthy were caught up in the morning rush toward another day at work. Their minds were on the morning news or the results of the last night's baseball games. They were sheltered, insulated from the drama that pierces every day in every hospital.

I stared at the clock again. The second hand was not moving in a smooth sweeping action around the face of the clock. This second hand moved with silent, distinct jerks from second to second. Each second was abrupt as if to announce every moment with punctuated clarity. Five-four-three-two-one—another minute had passed. The long minute hand was also moving, but its pace was so slow as to be almost imperceptible.

The rhythm of the clock signaled a growing alarm within me. My visceral reaction showed itself outwardly by sweating palms and an intense need to get up from my chair and pace the room. I had exhausted my interest in the magazines and grown weary of small talk with the strangers around me who were trying to mask their own anxiety.

The clock was telling a story. I did not like its message. The operation was taking too long. The preliminary diagnosis had been "routine." The surgery was to be corrective. There was no cause for alarm. This type of surgery was done countless times with no adverse results. But it was taking too long.

More time passed. By now I had memorized the brand name of the clock on the wall. The second hand kept jerking from one black mark between the numerals to the next.

At last the surgeon appeared. He was still dressed in his green uniform. "Mr. Sproul?" he asked. "Yes sir," I replied. "We ran into some complications. I'm afraid that we have discovered a tumor that we didn't expect. The final results will have to come from pathology, but there is little doubt that it is malignant."

His words were like a kick in the stomach. I didn't care about the clock anymore. I calmly asked the question that I wanted to scream: "What's the prognosis?"

"I'm afraid that it's not good. We can try chemotherapy, but to be frank, all we can really hope for is some time. This form of cancer is virulent. It is almost always fatal."

"How much time, Doctor?" I asked.

"We can never say for sure. Six months to a year. Perhaps more if the therapy is effective."

"Does she know?" was my next question.

"No, not yet. She's in the recovery room and is heavily sedated. I plan to tell her tomorrow. I would appreciate it if you could be with her when I give my report. I will be in about one."

"Of course. I will be there. I'm sure she will want to know the truth."

I had difficulty sleeping that night. I was frightened. My studies in theology gave me no practical knowledge about how to deal with such an illness. How do you announce to someone that they have a terminal illness? Do you disguise the truth? Shield the truth? Deny the truth? Do you hold out false hope? Do you promise a miracle that God may not be pleased to grant?

I approached my friend's room the next afternoon with apprehension. When I entered she was remarkably alert and outwardly serene. Her eyes told me, however, that somehow she already knew. I was spared any awkward questions as the doctor appeared almost immediately.

He was kind and gentle, yet forthright. "I don't like

what we found yesterday," he said. In quiet terms he explained exactly what it was. He set forth the procedures for chemotherapy. He explained the damage that was already done to vital organs.

I sensed that among the three of us in the room the patient had the calmest spirit. She spoke to comfort us. "It's all right," she said. "I'm ready for what God has in store for me."

My friend lived for two years, surprising everyone, including the doctors. She remained productive. She visited Israel. She got her house in order. She cared for her family. She died with grace and dignity.

During those two years we had many conversations. We prayed together. We cried together. We laughed together. She gave me elaborate instructions for her funeral. She discussed her will with me.

This woman was a Christian. She viewed her final months in this world as a vocation. She prepared herself mentally and spiritually for death. She viewed death as part of life. It was an experience she had never had before. It was the final experience of life that every person must undergo.

PART ONE

Suffering
and Death

CHAPTER ONE
THE FINAL CALLING

Dare we think of death as a *vocation*? The author of Ecclesiastes made this declaration:

To everything there is a season, a time for every purpose under heaven: a time to be born, and a time to die. Ecclesiastes 3:1-2a

Likewise the author of Hebrews says:

And as it is appointed for men to die once, but after this the judgment. Hebrews 9:27

Notice the language of Scripture. It speaks of death in terms of a "*purpose* under heaven" and of an "appointment." Death is a divine appointment. It is part of God's purpose in our lives. God calls each person to die. He is sovereign over all of life, including the final experience of life.

Usually we limit the idea of vocation to our careers or our jobs. The word *vocation*, however, comes from the Latin word *vocare*, meaning "to call." Used in the Christian sense, vocation refers to a divine calling, a summons that comes from God Himself. He calls people to teach, to preach, to sing, to make cars, and to change diapers. There are as many vocations as there are facets to human life.

We have different vocations with respect to jobs and tasks that God gives us in this life. But we all share in the vocation of death. Every one of us is called to die. That vocation is as much a calling from God as is a "call" to the ministry of Christ. Sometimes the call comes suddenly and without warning. Sometimes it comes with a notification in advance. But it comes to all of us. And it comes from God.

I am aware that there are teachers who tell us that God has nothing to do with death. Death is seen strictly as the fiendish device of the Devil. All pain, suffering, disease, and tragedy are blamed on the Evil One. God is absolved of any responsibility. This view is designed to make sure that God is absolved of blame for anything that goes wrong in this world. "God always wills healing," we are told. If that healing does not happen, then the fault lies with Satan—or with ourselves. Death, they say, is not in the plan of God. It represents a victory for Satan over the realm of God.

Such views may bring temporary relief to the

afflicted. But they are not true. They have nothing to do with biblical Christianity. In an effort to absolve God of any blame, they do so at the expense of God's sovereignty.

Yes, there is a Devil. He is our archenemy. He will do anything in his power to bring misery into our lives. But Satan is not sovereign. Satan does not hold the keys of death.

When Jesus appeared in a vision to John on the Isle of Patmos, He identified Himself with these words:

Do not be afraid; I am the First and the Last. I am He who lives, and was dead, and behold, I am alive forevermore. Amen. And I have the keys of Hades and of Death. Revelation 1:17-18

Jesus holds the keys to death. Satan cannot snatch those keys out of His hand. The grip of Christ is firm. He holds the keys because He owns the keys. All authority in heaven and on earth has been given to Him. That authority includes all authority over life and all authority over death. The angel of death is at His beck and call.

We remember the words of the great negro spiritual, "God's Trombones." Here the scenario is in heaven. The Lord speaks with the thunderous tones of divine authority. "Call Death!" He declares, "Send Death for Sister Caroline, down in Atlanta, Georgia."

The pale horse of the Apocalypse is summoned and dispatched by God, and by God alone.

World history has witnessed the emergence of many forms of religious dualism. Dualism affirms the existence of two equal and opposite forces. These forces are variously called Good and Evil, God and

Satan, Ying and Yang. The two forces are locked in
eternal combat. Since they are equal as well as
opposite, the conflict goes on forever, with neither side
ever gaining the upper hand. The world is doomed to
be forever the battleground between these hostile
forces. We are the victims of their struggle, the pawns
in their eternal chess game.

Dualism is on a collision course with Christianity.
The Christian faith has no stock in such a dualism.
Satan may be opposite to God, but he is by no means
equal. Satan is a creature; God is the Creator. Satan is
potent; God is omnipotent. Satan is knowledgeable
and crafty; God is omniscient. Satan is localized in his
presence; God is omnipresent. Satan is finite; God is
infinite. The list could continue. But it is clear from
Scripture that Satan is not an ultimate force in any
way.

We are not doomed to an ultimate conflict with no
hope of resolution. The message of Scripture is victory.
Full, final, and ultimate victory. It is not our doom
that is certain, but Satan's. His head has been crushed
by the heel of Christ. It is Christ who is Alpha and
Omega.

Above all suffering and death stands the crucified
and risen Lord. He has defeated the ultimate enemy of
life. He has vanquished the power of death. He calls us
to die, but that call is a call to obedience to the final
transition of life. Because of Christ, death is not final.
It is a passage from one world to the next.

God does not always will healing. If He did He
would suffer endless frustration from His plans that
are thwarted. He did not will the healing of Stephen
from the wounds inflicted by stones that were hurled
against him. He did not will the healing of Moses, of

Joseph, of David, of Paul, of Augustine, of Luther, of Calvin. These all died in faith.

To be sure, there is ultimate healing that comes through death and after death. Jesus was gloriously healed of the wounds of crucifixion, but only *after* He died.

Teachers argue that there is healing in the atonement of Christ. Indeed there is. Jesus bore all of our sins upon the cross. Yet none of us is free of sin in this life. None of us is free of sickness in this life. The healing that is in the cross is real. We participate in its benefits now, in this life. But the fullness of the healing of both sin and disease takes place in heaven. We still must die when it is our appointed time.

Certainly God answers prayers and gives healings to our bodies during this life. But even these healings are temporary. Jesus raised Lazarus from the dead. But Lazarus died again. Jesus gave sight to the blind and hearing to the deaf. Yet every person Jesus healed eventually died. They died not because Satan finally won over Jesus, but because Jesus called them to die.

When God issues a call upon us it is always a holy call. The vocation of dying is a sacred vocation. To understand that is one of the most important lessons a Christian can ever learn. When the summons comes we can respond in many ways. We can be angry, bitter, or terrified. But if we see it as a call from God and not a threat from Satan, we are far more able to cope with its difficulties.

Finishing the Race

I will never forget the last words my father spoke to me. We were seated together on the living room sofa.

His body had been ravaged by three strokes. One side of his face was distorted by paralysis. His left eye and left lip drooped uncontrollably. He spoke to me with a heavy slur. His words were difficult to understand, but their meaning was crystal clear. He uttered these words: "I have fought the good fight, I have finished the race. I have kept the faith."

These were the last words he ever spoke to me. Hours later he suffered his fourth and final cerebral hemorrhage. I found him collapsed on the floor, a trickle of blood oozing from the corner of his mouth. He was comatose. Mercifully, he died a day and a half later without regaining consciousness.

His last words to me were heroic. My last words to him were cowardly. I protested his words of premonition. I said rudely, "Don't say that, Dad!"

There are many things that I have said in my life that I desperately wished I had not said. None of my words are more shameful to me now than those. But words can no more be recalled than a speeding arrow after the bow string has snapped in full release.

My words were a rebuke to him. I refused to allow him the dignity of a final testimony to me. He knew he was dying. I refused to accept what he had already accepted with grace.

I was seventeen. I knew nothing of the business of dying. It was not a very good year. I watched my father die an inch at a time over a period of three years. I never heard him complain. I never heard him protest. He sat in the same chair day after day, week after week, year after year. He read the Bible with a large magnifying glass. I was blind to the anxieties that must have plagued him. He could not work. There was no income. No disability insurance. He sat there, waiting to die, watching his life savings trickle away with his own life.

I was angry at God. My father was angry at no one. He lived out his last days faithful to his vocation. He fought the good fight. A good fight is a fight fought without hostility, without bitterness, without self-pity. I had never been in a fight like that.

My father finished the race. I was not even in the starting blocks. He ran the race for which God had called him. He ran until his legs crumbled. But somehow he kept going. When he couldn't walk anymore he still was at the table each night for dinner. He asked me to help him. It was a daily ritual. Each evening I went to his room where he was seated in that same chair. I stooped backward, facing away from him so that he could drape his arms around my neck and shoulders. I clasped his wrists together and lifted my body, bringing him up from the chair. Then I dragged him, fireman style, to the dining room table. He finished the race. My only consolation is that I was able to help him. I was with him at the finish line.

I carried him one last time. When I found him unconscious on the floor, somehow I managed to get him into the bed where he died. On that trip he could not help me drag him. He could not put his arms around my neck. It took effort mixed with adrenalin to get him from the floor to the bed. But I had to get him there. It was unthinkable to me that he should die on the floor.

When my father died I was not a Christian. Faith was something beyond my experience and beyond my understanding. When he said, "I have kept the faith," I missed the weight of his words. I shut them out. I had no idea that he was quoting the apostle Paul's final message to his beloved disciple, Timothy. His eloquent testimony was wasted on me at the time. But not now. Now I understand. Now I want to persevere as he persevered. I want to run the race and finish the course as he did before me. I have no desire to suffer as he suffered. But I want to keep the faith as he kept it.

If my father taught me anything, he taught me how to die. The events I have just described have left an indelible mark upon me. For years after my father died I had the same recurring nightmare. I dreamed the same dream. The dream had a vivid intensity. I would see my father alive again. The beginning of the dream was thrilling. In my slumber the impossible became real. He was alive! But my joy would change quickly to despair as his appearance in my dream was always the same. He was crippled. He was paralyzed. He was hopelessly and helplessly dying. The scene was never of a healthy, vibrant father, but of a father caught in the throes of death.

I would wake up sweating with a sick empty feeling in the pit of my stomach. Only as I studied the Scriptures did I discover that death is not like that. Only when I discovered the content of the Christian faith did the nightmares finally cease.

Passing through the Valley of the Shadow

I met a young lady whose mother had recently died. She had been grieving deeply, assaulted by attacks of despair. She had a morbid preoccupation with her mother's death. Then, one evening, she had a profound spiritual experience. She was alone, meditating on the words of Scripture. Suddenly she experienced a profound sense of the presence of God.

As she prayed, some words thrust themselves forcibly into her mind. They were strong words. Emphatic. The words that were impressed on her brain were these: "Leslie! Death's not like that!"

The grief was over. Leslie was delivered from her morbid spirit. A flash of understanding rescued her soul. A new view of death was born in her understanding.

When God gives us a vocation to die, He sends us on a mission. We are indeed entered into a race. The course may be frightening. It is an obstacle course with pitfalls in the way. We wonder if we will have the courage to make our way to the finish line. The trail takes us through the valley of the shadow.

The valley of the shadow of death. It is a valley where the sun's rays often seem to be blotted out. To approach it is to tremble. We would prefer to walk around it, to seek a safe bypass. But men and women of faith can enter that valley without fear. David told us how:

Yea, though I walk through the valley of the shadow of death, I will fear no evil; for You are with me; Your rod and Your staff, they comfort me. Psalm 23:4

David was a shepherd. In this psalm David puts himself in the place of the sheep. He sees himself as a lamb under the care of the Great Shepherd. He enters the valley without fear for one overarching reason: the Shepherd goes with him. He trusts himself to the care and the protection of the Shepherd.

The lamb finds comfort in the Shepherd's weapons, the rod and the staff. The ancient shepherd was armed. He would use the crook of his staff to rescue a fallen lamb from a pit. He would wield his rod against hostile beasts that sought to devour his sheep. Without the shepherd the sheep would be helpless in the shadowy valley. But as long as the shepherd was present the lamb had nothing to fear.

If a bear or lion attacked the shepherd and killed the shepherd, the sheep would scatter. They would be vulnerable to the lion's jaws. If the shepherd fell, all would be lost for the sheep.

But we have a Shepherd who cannot fall. We have a Shepherd who cannot die. He is no hireling who abandons his flock at the first sign of trouble. Our Shepherd is armed with omnipotent force. He is not threatened by the valley of shadows. He created the valley. He redeems the valley.

David's confidence was rooted in the absolute certainty of the presence of God. He understood that with a Divine vocation comes Divine assistance and the absolute promise of Divine presence. God will not send us where He refuses to go Himself.

My best friend in college and seminary was a man named Don McClure. Don was the son of pioneer missionaries. He had grown up in the remote interior of Africa. Don personally discovered several tribes of primitive natives for whom he was the first white man they had ever seen. He had killed spitting cobras in his bedroom. He had a close encounter with a crocodile that had literally jumped into his small canoe with him. He had been rescued by his father at the last minute when he was surrounded by a hungry pride of lions.

I called Don "Tarzan" because his life mirrored the legends of Johnny Weismuller. He was the most fearless person I ever met. I always said that if I were trapped in a foxhole behind enemy lines in combat, the one man I would want with me is Don McClure.

I keep a newspaper clipping in my Bible that reports the martyrdom of Don's father. A few years ago Don and his father were camped in a remote area of Ethiopia. During the night they were awakened by a surprise attack from Communist guerrillas. Don and his father were captured and dragged before a firing squad. Don stood next to his father when the guerrillas opened fire. First they shot Don's dad, killing him instantly. Don heard the shot and saw the flame from the rifle that was pointed at him from six feet away. He fell next to his father, shocked to realize that he was still alive.

In the confusion of the night the guerrillas fled as quickly as they had appeared. Don hugged the ground, feigning death until all was quiet. He had suffered only minor flesh wounds though he was covered with powder burns. Fighting the impulse to flee, Don remained long enough to dig a shallow grave with his bare hands. There he committed his father's body to the ground.

Don survived. His father didn't. I still would be proud to have Don McClure at my side in the valley of the shadow. But I have one greater than Don who promises to go with me.

The presence of God is our refuge and our strength in times of trouble. His promise is not only to go with us into the valley. Even more important is His promise of what lies on the other side of the valley. God promises to go with us for the entire journey to guide us to what lies beyond. The valley of the shadow of death is not a box canyon. It is open-ended. It is a passageway to a better country. The valley leads to life—life far more abundant than anything we can imagine. The goal of our vocation is heaven. But there is no route to heaven except through the valley.

David also understood that. Though he lived before Christ, before the Resurrection, before the New Testament revelation of glory, nevertheless God had not been altogether silent on the matter. Already there was the hope of the bosom of Abraham.

David confessed his faith in this manner:

I would have lost heart, unless I had believed that I would see the goodness of the LORD in the land of the living. Psalm 27:13

The God of Abraham, Isaac, and Jacob is the God of the living. The God of David is the God of the living. The God of Jesus is the God of the living. There is life beyond the shadow of death.

My father ran a race because God called him to run the race. He finished the course because God was with him through every obstacle. He kept the faith because the faith kept him.

This was a powerful legacy. It is the legacy the risen Christ gives to His sheep.

CHAPTER TWO
WALKING THE VIA DOLOROSA

"He began to be sorrowful and deeply distressed" (Matthew 26:37).

Sorrow and deep distress marked the inner spirit of Jesus as He entered into prayer in the Garden of Gethsemane. This moment marked a time of intense agony for Him. He was nearing the climax of His Great Passion. The Great Passion of Jesus was the focal point of His divine vocation. No one was ever called by God to greater suffering than that suffering to which God called His only begotten Son.

Our Savior was a suffering Savior. He went before us into the uncharted land of agony and death. He went where no man is called to go. His Father gave Him a cup to drink that will never touch our lips. We will not ever be asked of God to endure anything comparable to the distress Christ took upon Himself. Wherever God calls us to go, whatever He summons us to endure will fall far short of what Jesus experienced.

From the beginning of His ministry Jesus was conscious of His mission. From the start He was under a death sentence. His "disease" was terminal. The Father afflicted Him on the cross, not with one terminal disease, but with every terminal disease. Of course, this does not mean that Jesus received a positive biopsy report or that a physician diagnosed Him with advanced leprosy. He went to His death with no outward evidence of any known disease. But the cumulative pain of every disease was laid upon Him. He bore in His body the ravages of every evil, every sickness, every pain known to the human race.

The suffering of Jesus was multiple because the extent of evil in the world is a vast complex. Every effect of every sin was placed upon Him. To carry this dreadful burden was His vocation. To bear all pain and disease was His mission. The magnitude of this horror is beyond our understanding. But He understood it because it was His to bear.

The Scandal of a Suffering Christ

That the Son of God should suffer was unthinkable to many of His contemporaries. To the Greeks it was a stumbling block. Their idea of God was so spiritual, so ethereal, that they had no room for the concept of Incarnation. God could never be involved with physical suffering simply because God could never be involved with anything physical.

The scandalous news of the New Testament is that God became incarnate. The eternal, divine Word was made flesh. That flesh was vulnerable to all physical torment.

Yet it was not only the Greeks who were scandalized by such a thought. That God should appear in human form was thinkable to the Jews. But that the humanness could actually suffer was beyond their comprehension.

Following the moment of Peter's greatest confession at Caesarea Philippi came one of the sharpest rebukes he ever heard from Jesus. In answer to Jesus' question, "Who do you say that I am?" (Matthew 16:15), Simon Peter replied, "You are the Christ, the Son of the living God" (Matthew 16:16).

For this response Peter received the benediction of Jesus:

Blessed are you, Simon Bar-Jonah, for flesh and blood has not revealed this to you, but my Father who is in heaven. And I also say to you that you are Peter, and on this rock I will build My church, and the gates of Hades shall not prevail against it. Matthew 16:17-18

What higher commendation could a man receive than to receive such a blessing from Christ Himself? Yet moments later this same man received a stinging rebuke from Jesus:

Get behind Me, Satan: You are an offense to Me, for you are not mindful of the things of God, but the things of men. Matthew 16:23

These words were spoken not to Satan but to Peter. The dialogue here is volatile. One moment Jesus puts His benediction upon Simon Peter, and the next moment He calls him "Satan." How can we explain this dramatic shift in tone and words? Jesus was not given to undue severity in His treatment of people. Neither was He two-faced, praising with one side of His mouth and cursing with the other.

This shift of speech must be understood in light of the interval that passed between commendation and rebuke. The interval contained an exchange between Peter and Jesus regarding suffering:

From that time Jesus began to show to His disciples that He must go to Jerusalem, and suffer many things from the elders and chief priests and scribes, and be killed, and be raised again the third day.
Matthew 16:21

We notice here that Jesus was showing that He *must* suffer and die. His trip to Jerusalem was not optional. He had a destiny to fulfill, a rendezvous on Golgotha. This "mustness" was rooted in His vocation. He was called to perform a task. It was His duty to suffer and die.

It was precisely at this point of duty that Peter challenged Him: "Then Peter took Him aside and began to rebuke Him, saying, 'Far be it from You, Lord; this shall not happen to you!'" (Matthew 16:22).

At least Peter had the grace to rebuke his Lord privately. He didn't flaunt his arrogance publicly, though the Holy Spirit has entered his unspeakable presumption in the public record of Scripture.

"Far be it from you, Lord." Peter demanded that Jesus distance Himself from suffering and death. Jesus recognized in this demand the same seductive suggestion that Satan offered in the wilderness. Peter wanted a Savior unsullied by suffering. He wanted the Kingdom to come Satan's way rather than God's way. God's way was the way of the cross, the *Via Dolorosa*.

Theologians argue about when in Jesus' life it entered His consciousness that He must suffer and die. The Bible makes it clear that the idea was formulated long before Caesarea Philippi. The concept was foreshadowed as early as Genesis 3:15: "And I will put enmity between you and the woman, and between your seed and her Seed; He shall bruise your head, and you shall bruise His heel." This is the Protevangelium, the first hint of the gospel that was to come.

The idea of a suffering Messiah was greatly expanded in the Suffering Servant motif of Isaiah. It was prophesied to Mary by the venerable prophet Simeon in the temple: "Behold, this Child is destined for the fall and rising of many in Israel, and for a sign which will be spoken against (yes, a sword will pierce through your own soul also), that the thoughts of many hearts may be revealed" (Luke 2:34-35).

We don't know exactly when Jesus became aware of His destiny, but His mother received a foreshadowing of a piercing sword in the first weeks of His life. At age twelve Jesus declared that He *must* be about His Father's business. By then He was aware of a *mustness,* a duty that was His to perform. Whether He realized the full import of that duty at such an early age is a matter of conjecture. But certainly by the time He arrived at the Garden of Gethsemane it was no surprise.

In the Garden He entered into His sorrow. He said to His disciples, "My soul is exceedingly sorrowful, even to death. Stay here and watch with Me" (Matthew 26:38).

The Scriptures tell us that after saying these words Jesus went farther into the olive grove and fell on His face as He prayed: "O My Father, if it is possible, let this cup pass from Me; nevertheless, not as I will, but as You will" (Matthew 26:39). Luke adds to the historical record these words: "And being in agony, He prayed more earnestly. And His sweat became like great drops of blood falling down to the ground" (Luke 22:44).

Accepting God's "No" as God's Will

We are astonished that in the light of such clear biblical records anyone would ever have the audacity to suggest that it is wrong for the afflicted in body or soul to couch their prayers for deliverance in terms of "If it be thy will." We are told that when affliction comes God always wills healing. That He has nothing to do with suffering, that all we must do is claim the answer we seek by faith. We are exhorted to claim God's "Yes" before He speaks it.

Away with such distortions of biblical faith! They are conceived in the mind of the Tempter who would seduce us into changing faith into magic. No amount of pious verbiage can transform such falsehood into sound doctrine.

God sometimes says no. Sometimes He calls us to suffer and die even if we want to claim the contrary. Never did a man pray more earnestly than Christ prayed in Gethsemane. Who will charge Jesus with failure to pray in faith? He put His request before the Father with sweat of blood: "Let this cup pass from me."

Jesus' prayer was straightforward and without ambiguity. He cried out for relief. He asked for the horribly bitter cup to be removed. Every ounce of His humanness shrank from the cup. He begged the Father to relieve Him of His duty. But God said no. The way of suffering was the Father's plan. It was the Father's will. It was His pure unadulterated will. The cross was not Satan's idea. The passion of Christ was not the result of human contingency. It was not the accidental contrivance of Caiaphas, Herod, or Pilate. The cup was prepared, delivered, and administered by Almighty God.

Jesus qualified His prayer: "If it be thy will . . . " Jesus did not "name it and claim it." He knew His Father well enough to know that it might not be His will. The story does not end with the words, "And the Father repented of the evil He had planned, removed the cup, and Jesus lived happily ever after."

Such words border on blasphemy. The gospel is not a fairy tale. The Father would not negotiate the cup. Jesus was called to drink it to its last dregs. And He accepted it. "Nevertheless, not My will, but Yours, be done" (Luke 22:42).

This "nevertheless" was the supreme prayer of faith. The prayer of faith is not a demand that we place upon God. It is not a presumption of a granted request. The authentic prayer of faith is one that models Jesus' prayer. It is always uttered in a spirit of subordination. In all our prayers we must let God be God. No one tells the Father what to do, nay, not even the Son. Prayers are always to be requests made in humility and submission to the Father's will.

The prayer of faith is a prayer of trust. The very essence of faith is trust. We trust that God knows what is best. The spirit of trust includes a spirit of willingness to do what the Father wants us to do. That kind of trust was embodied by Christ in Gethsemane.

Though the text is not explicit, it is clear that Jesus left the garden with the Father's answer to His plea. There was no cursing or bitterness. His meat and His drink were to do the Father's will. Once the Father said no, it was settled. Jesus prepared Himself for the cross. He did not flee from Jerusalem but entered the city with His face set like a flint.

Redeeming Through Suffering

In the life and passion of Christ we see most clearly that suffering is the way God has chosen to bring redemption to a fallen world. Jesus was known as a man of sorrows, acquainted with grief. His life and ministry followed in detail the mission set forth by Isaiah of the Suffering Servant of the Lord.

We read a fascinating story in the Book of Acts:

Now an angel of the Lord spoke to Philip saying, "Arise and go toward the south along the road which goes down from Jerusalem to Gaza." This is desert.

So he arose and went. And behold, a man of Ethiopia, a eunuch of great authority under Candace the queen of the Ethiopians, who had charge of all her treasury and had come to Jerusalem to worship, was returning. And sitting in his chariot, he was reading Isaiah the prophet.

Then the Spirit said to Philip, "Go near and overtake this chariot."

So Philip ran to him and heard him reading the prophet Isaiah, and said, "Do you understand what you are reading?" And he said, "How can I, unless someone guides me?" And he asked Philip to come up and sit with him.

The place in Scripture which he read was this:

"He was led as a sheep to the slaughter; and like a lamb silent before its shearer, so He opened not His mouth. In His humiliation His justice was taken away. And who will declare His generation? For His life is taken from the earth."

So the eunuch answered Philip and said, "I ask you of whom does the prophet say this, of himself or of some other man?"

Then Philip opened his mouth, and beginning at this Scripture, preached Jesus to him. Acts 8:26-35

Who is the Servant of the Lord? The Ethiopian eunuch asked Philip a crucial question. He had been reading from Isaiah 53 and was puzzled. His question is pivotal: "Of whom does the prophet say this, of himself or of some other man?"

Philip's answer was directly to the point. Isaiah was talking about Jesus.

The point may seem so obvious to the reader that one wonders why I take time to expand upon it. That the New Testament identifies Jesus with the Suffering Servant of Israel should be so obvious as to eliminate the need for discussion.

But it matters. It matters profoundly. Not only is our understanding of Jesus tied to this question, but the agonizing question of the meaning of our own suffering is tied to this.

I do not think it is an overstatement to declare that

the New Testament portrait of Jesus stands or falls with this issue.

In modern times we have seen a kind of biblical scholarship that considers all references of Jesus to Isaiah's Suffering Servant as contrived inventions of the New Testament writers. In a word, the charge is that the biblical writers fraudulently "doctored" the history of Jesus. After Jesus suffered and died, the early church had to invent an explanation for all this suffering. Therefore they created this link between Isaiah's Suffering Servant and Jesus. Then they put words into Jesus' mouth that He never uttered.

The critics have an ax to grind against the biblical view of Christ. Their ax is so heavy that they bump themselves in the head with it. If we know anything of the historical Jesus we know Him as one who suffered and died as the Servant of God.

In Luke's Gospel Jesus utters these words:

For I say to you that this which is written must still be accomplished in Me: "And He was numbered with the transgressors." For the things concerning me have an end. Luke 22:37

Here Jesus quotes directly from Isaiah 53. He identifies Himself with the Suffering Servant of God. The nation of Israel was called to be a suffering servant. That vocation was then personalized and crystallized in one man who represented Israel. Philip's answer was clear: That man was Jesus.

Jesus suffers "for us." Yet we are called to participate in His suffering. Though He was uniquely the fulfillment of Isaiah's prophecy, there is still an application of this vocation to us. We are given both the duty and the privilege to participate in the suffering of Christ.

A mysterious reference to this idea is found in the writings of the Apostle Paul:

I now rejoice in my sufferings for you, and fill up in my flesh what is lacking in the afflictions of Christ, for the sake of His body, which is the church.
Colossians 1:24

Here Paul declares that he rejoices in his suffering. Surely he does not mean that he enjoys pain and affliction. Rather, the cause of his joy is found in the meaning of his suffering. He says that he "fills up what is lacking in the afflictions of Christ."

On the surface Paul's explanation is astonishing. What could possibly be lacking in the afflictions of Christ? Did Christ only half finish His redemptive work only to wait for Paul to complete it? Was Jesus overstating the case when He cried from the cross, "It is finished"?

What exactly was lacking in the suffering of Christ? In terms of the *value* of Jesus' suffering it is blasphemous to suggest anything was lacking. The merit of His atoning sacrifice is infinite. Nothing could possibly be added to His perfect obedience to be even more perfect. Nothing can be more perfect than perfect. What is absolutely perfect can be neither augmented nor diminished.

The merit of Jesus is sufficient to atone for every sin that has ever been or ever will be committed. His atoning death needs no repetition for His deed once-for-all. Old Testament sacrifices were repeated precisely because they were imperfect shadows of the reality that was to come.

It was not by accident that the Roman Catholic Church appealed to Paul's words in this text to support their concept of a treasury of merits, by which the merits of the saints are added to the merit of Christ to cover the deficiencies of sinners. This doctrine was at the eye of the Protestant Reformation tornado. It was this eclipsing of the sufficiency and perfection of Christ's suffering that was at the heart of Martin Luther's protest.

Though we vigorously deny Rome's interpretation of this passage we are still left with our question. If Paul's suffering does not add merit to what is lacking in Christ's sufferings, what then does it add?

Adding in Our Own Sufferings

The answer to this difficult question lies in the broader teaching of the New Testament of the believer's call to participate in the humiliation of Christ. Our very baptism signifies that we are buried with Christ. Paul repeatedly points out that unless we are willing to participate in the humiliation of Jesus we will not participate in His exaltation. (See 2 Timothy 2:11-12.)

Paul rejoiced that his own suffering was a benefit to the church. The church is called to imitate Christ. It is called to walk the *via dolorosa*. Paul's favorite metaphor for the church was the image of the human body. The church is called the Body of Christ. In one sense it is proper to call the church the "Continuing Incarnation." The church is really the mystical body of Christ on earth.

Christ so linked His church to Himself that when He

first called Paul on the Damascus Road He said, "Saul, Saul, why do you persecute Me?" Saul was not persecuting Jesus. Jesus had already ascended to heaven. He was already out of reach of Paul's hostility. Saul was busy persecuting Christians. But Jesus saw such a relationship of solidarity with His church that He regarded an attack upon His body, the church, as a personal attack on Himself.

The church belongs to Christ. The church is redeemed by Christ. The church is the Bride of Christ. The church is indwelt by Christ. But the church is not Christ. Christ is perfect; the church is imperfect. Christ is the Redeemer; the church is the company of the redeemed.

The church participates in Christ's suffering. But this participation adds no merit to Christ's merit. The sufferings of Christians may benefit other people but they always fall short of atonement. I cannot atone for anyone's sins, not even for my own. Yet my suffering may be of great benefit to other people. It may also serve as a witness to the One whose sufferings were an atonement.

The word for "witness" in the New Testament, *martus,* is the word from which we get the English word *martyr.* Those who suffered and died for the cause of Christ were called martyrs because by their suffering they bore witness to Christ.

What is lacking in the afflictions of Jesus is the ongoing suffering which God calls His people to endure. God calls people of every generation to fulfill His divine plan of redemption. Again this suffering is not to fulfill any deficiency in the merit of Christ but to fulfill our destinies as witnesses to the perfect Suffering Servant of God.

What does this mean in practical terms? Let me return to the illustration of my own father. I'm sure that while he was suffering he must have asked God the question, "Why?" On the surface his suffering seemed useless. It seemed as though his pain was for no good reason.

Now I must be very careful. I do not think that my father's suffering was in any way an atonement for my sins. Nor do I think I can read God's mind with respect to the ultimate reason for my father's suffering. But I know this: My father's suffering made a profound impact on my life. It was through my father's death that I was brought to Christ. I am not saying that the ultimate reason my father was called to suffer and die was so that I could become a Christian. I don't know the sovereign purpose of God in it. But I do know that God *used* that suffering in a redemptive way for me. My dad's suffering drove me into the arms of the Suffering Savior.

We are followers of Christ. We follow Him to the Garden of Gethsemane. We follow Him into the Hall of Judgment. We follow Him along the *Via Dolorosa*. We follow Him unto death. But the gospel declares, we follow Him through the gates of Heaven. Because we suffer with Him, we shall also be raised with Him. If we are humiliated with Him we shall also be exalted with Him.

It is because of Christ that our suffering is not useless. It is part of the total plan of God who has chosen to redeem the world through the pathway of suffering.

CHAPTER THREE

A CASE STUDY IN SUFFERING

The vice president of operations of a large corporation became intensely jealous of a district manager in the company. The district manager enjoyed a close personal relationship with the chairman of the board. Moved by his jealousy, the vice president lodged a complaint with the chairman.

"I think we ought to get rid of Hawkins," he suggested. The chairman replied, "Why? He's one of the most productive managers we have. I think he's doing an outstanding job. And besides, he is the most loyal employee we have."

"Loyal? You think he's loyal? No wonder he's

loyal," the vice president said with dripping cynicism. "He's always buttering you up. He's only loyal because you pay him such a high salary. You give him benefits that no one else receives. Besides, you've built a wall of protection around him. Everybody knows that he's your fair-haired boy. I wonder how loyal he'd be if you put the heat on him. Cut his salary and see how loyal he would be."

The chairman was irritated by this suggestion, but he responded to the challenge. "All right. Let's see about it. Go ahead and cut his salary. Put some heat on. I think you will see that Hawkins will maintain his loyalty."

The vice president gave a sarcastic laugh. "You just let me at him and he'll betray you and the company in a minute."

The vice president left the board room and put together a scheme to bring Hawkins crashing down. First, he cut his salary in half. Then he approached some of Hawkins's coworkers and enlisted them in his scheme. They were eager to join in. They gleefully contrived plans of industrial sabotage to destroy Hawkins's productivity record. They falsified reports and covertly disrupted some of the machinery in the plant. Suddenly Hawkins's plant was besieged with customer complaints about poor quality control.

The heat was on. The vice president and his henchmen referred to the district manager as "Stainless Steel" Hawkins. "Hawkins is a holy Joe. He thinks he's better than anybody else. It's time he got what he really deserves."

Hawkins took it in stride. He worked even harder to solve the mysterious rash of problems that had arisen. This merely fueled the antagonism of his enemies.

They began to put more pressure on. "Accidents" began to happen in the plant. The conspirators started to harass Hawkins's family. To make matters worse, Hawkins suddenly became ill. Even his illness was of a suspicious origin. The vice president went so far as to bribe a corrupt physician to introduce a virile strand of bacteria into Hawkins's diet. Joe Hawkins's world began to fall apart. His sickness was taking its toll. Coupled with the plunging production of his plant, Hawkins's star began to fade. Some of his closest friends came to him with sharp criticism. "What's wrong with you, Hawkins? You've lost something. Your performance is down. No wonder they cut your salary."

Hawkins's friends began to think that their former opinion of him was wrong. They assumed that somehow Hawkins must have done something really bad for his life to have taken such a sudden and drastic turn for the worse. One of his friends even came to him with "spiritual" counsel. "Joe," he said, "I need to tell you something in love. The troubles you've been having must come from God. I think it is a kind of punishment for unconfessed sin in your life. Maybe if you repent things will start to go better for you."

"Maybe you're right," Joe Hawkins replied, "but I'm not aware of anything I've done to deserve this, but I will certainly search my soul about it."

"But even the chairman cut your salary in half. Doesn't that tell you something?"

"Well, the chairman has a right to do that. He's always been fair with me. I'm sure he knows what he is doing. He must have a good reason for his action," Joe answered.

Then Joe's wife got into the act. "Honey," she said

one evening, "I think it's time for you to resign. Your health is failing and the company is treating you like dirt. After all your years of faithful service, this is the thanks you get. Let's get out and start over somewhere else. You're crazy to keep working for a company like this."

"No, Hon," Joe answered. "I can't leave."

"Why not?" his wife demanded.

"I owe it to the chairman of the board to stay on."

"Are you crazy? You don't owe him anything. You've given him the best years of your life, and now this. He owes you! You don't owe him a thing. Why don't you face it, Joe, the chairman's as rotten as the deal he's given you."

"No!" Joe snapped in anger. "I just can't believe that he would treat me unfairly on purpose."

"Then you'd better talk to him face to face. I'd love to hear what he says when you confront him."

"OK, OK, I'll talk to him," Joe promised.

The next day Joe made an appointment to see the chairman. When he was ushered into the teak-paneled office the chairman greeted him in a friendly manner. "Hi, Joe. What can I do for you?"

Joe got straight to the point. He gushed out his grievances in a torrent of rage. "What's going on here?" he demanded. "You've cut my salary in half. You stand by and let a bunch of thieves sabotage my plant. You don't give me any health benefits. What did I do to deserve this kind of treatment? I've been loyal to you and to the company for years and now you treat me like this. Who do you think you are, anyway?"

The chairman listened patiently to Joe's diatribe. Then he responded. "Let me ask you some questions, Joe. Do you own this company?"

"No, sir," Joe replied.

"Did you build this place from scratch? Did you risk your own capital in this operation? Do you pay all the bills? Are you the chairman of the board?"

To all these questions Joe sat shaking his head, "No."

"Tell me, Joe, who are you to tell me how to run my company? I've given you everything I ever promised you and more. Look at your contract. Does your contract specify that you should receive all the bonuses I've given you over the years?"

Again Joe had to give an honest answer. "No, sir, you really have been more than kind to me."

"Have I, Joe? Do you think I've changed? Do you think I'm not aware of what's going on here? I know you have been treated unfairly. I know exactly what's going on in that plant. I've been studying the matter carefully. Nothing has escaped my notice. Joe, I'm going to ask you to do something for me. You've trusted me in the past. Trust me now. It may take some time but I guarantee you that I will straighten things out. But you have to be patient. I have a plan. Those who have plotted against you will get everything they deserve. Do you really think I would let them get away with this?"

Joe felt awful. He began to stammer an apology. "I'm sorry," he said. "I had no right to come in there and lay all these accusations on you. I've complained once. But no more. You'll never hear another word of protest out of my mouth. Do whatever you will. I trust you."

The chairman smiled. He spoke into the intercom to his secretary. "Mrs. Franklin, have the vice president of operations report to my office immediately. I'm giving him his walking papers."

"Don't leave yet, Joe. I have a few words for you. First, I want you to know that beginning tomorrow morning you will be elevated to a vice presidency in the company. You will receive double the salary you had before your pay was cut. Even at this hour a physician is on his way from Atlanta with a special vaccine that will cure your disease. You have been loyal to me, Joe, more loyal than any other employee. You've endured a lot without cursing me behind my back. Now it is time for you to be vindicated."

"I knew it," exclaimed Joe. "I must admit I had my moments of doubt, but deep down inside I knew you would fix everything. Now I really feel embarrassed for all those accusations I made to you. How can you ever forgive me?"

"Joe, don't worry about it. That's one thing I know how to do. Forgive. I major in forgiveness."

Is There a Connection of Sin with Suffering?

Surely by now the reader has recognized that this is the story of the biblical character Job, thinly disguised in modern garb. The story of Job is a case study in human suffering. It chronicles the drama of a righteous man who underwent extreme misery in this world. His misery was compounded by his friends' insensitivity toward him. They made an assumption that the Bible forbids. They assumed that Job's degree of suffering was in direct proportion to his sin. They assumed that there is a ratio in this world between suffering and guilt. Since Job's suffering was great, it must have been a sign that his sin was equally great.

God does not allow this equation. We remember the

question put to Jesus about the man who was born blind:

Now as Jesus passed by, He saw a man who was blind from birth. And His disciples asked Him, saying, "Rabbi, who sinned, this man or his parents, that he was born blind?" Jesus answered, "Neither this man nor his parents sinned, but that the works of God should be revealed in him." John 9:1-3

In the science of logic there is an informal fallacy called the fallacy of the false dilemma. Sometimes it is called the either/or fallacy. This error of reasoning occurs when a problem is presented as if it allowed only two possible explanations when in reality there are three or more options.

Some issues are indeed of an either/or character. For example, either there is a God or there is not. There is no third option. But because some questions may be reduced to only two alternatives does not mean that all questions may be so reduced. This is the error the disciples made concerning the man born blind.

When the disciples considered the plight of the blind man they assumed there were only two possible explanations for it. Either the blindness was a direct result of the man's own sin or it was the result of his parents' sin.

Their thinking was wrong, but it was not utterly groundless. They were correct in one assumption. They knew enough about Scripture to realize that there is a connection between suffering and sin. They understood that suffering and death entered the world because of sin. Before sin entered the world there was no suffering or death.

Death is unnatural. It may be natural to fallen man,

but it was not natural to man as he was created. Man was not created to die. He was created with the possibility of death but not with the necessity of death. Death was introduced as a consequence of sin. If there is no sin, there is no death. But when sin entered, the curse of the Fall was added. All death and suffering flow out of the complex of sin.

The disciples were partially correct at another point. They were aware that sometimes there is a direct link between a person's sin and his suffering. God afflicted Miriam with leprosy as a judgment upon her for her sin against Moses (Numbers 12:9-10).

The error of the disciples was in assuming that there is *always* a direct correlation, a fixed ratio between a person's suffering and a person's sin. In this world there are times when a person suffers far less than what is merited for one's sins, while others endure a greater proportion of suffering. This disparity is seen in David's cry, "LORD, how long will the wicked, how long will the wicked triumph?" (Psalm 94:3).

There are times when we suffer innocently at other people's hands. When that occurs we are victims of injustice. But that injustice is at a horizontal level. No one suffers injustice on a vertical level. That is, no one ever suffers unjustly in terms of our relationship with God. As long as we bear the guilt of sin we cannot protest that God is unjust in allowing us to suffer.

If someone wrongfully causes me to suffer, I have every right to plead with God for vindication even as Job did. Yet at the same time I must not complain to God that He is at fault in allowing this suffering to befall me. In terms of my relationship to other people I may be innocent, but in terms of my relationship to God I am not an innocent victim. It is one thing for me to ask God for justice in my dealings with men. It is another thing for me to demand justice in my relationship with God. No more perilous demand could be uttered than for a sinner to demand justice from God. The worst thing that could possibly befall me is to receive pure justice from God.

"God Meant It for Good"

All of these considerations aside, the fact remains that the disciples still committed the fallacy of the false dilemma. They limited the reason for the man's blindness to two possible explanations (the man's own sin or his parents') when there was at least one other explanation for the blindness that they failed to consider.

Jesus punctured the false dilemma by saying, "Neither!" The reason why the man was born blind was *not* because of his sin. Nor was it because of his parents' sin. Jesus declared that the man was born blind so "that the works of God should be revealed in him."

The man born blind was afflicted with blindness for the glory of God. This is the startling conclusion our Lord revealed. This is a crucial teaching for us. It serves as a warning for us not to jump to conclusions about the "why" of our suffering.

God used the man's blindness for His greater glory. Here the "evil" of disease and suffering is made serviceable to God. He triumphs over it and brings His glorious plan to pass through it. We remember the dreadful suffering of Joseph at the hands of his brothers. Yet because of their treachery the plan of God for all of history was brought to pass.

At the moment of Joseph's reconciliation with his brothers, he exclaimed, "But as for you, you meant evil against me; but God meant it for good, in order to bring it about as it is this day, to save many people alive" (Genesis 50:20).

Here we see God working through evil to effect salvation. It does not make the evil of Joseph's brothers any less evil. Judas's betrayal was a wicked act. It brought unjust suffering upon Jesus even as Joseph was a victim of his brothers' injustice. But over all injustice, all pain, all suffering stands a sovereign God who works His plan of salvation *over, against,* and even *through* evil.

Trusting No Matter What

What Jesus declared to His disciples about the blind man is clearly displayed in the Book of Job. Had the disciples mastered this Old Testament book, perhaps they would not have fallen into the either/or fallacy. Their mistake was the same mistake committed by Job's friends.

Job protested the words of his friends. His reply is poignant:

I have heard many such things: Miserable comforters are you all! Shall words of wind have an end? Or what provokes you that you answer? I could also speak as you do, if your soul were in my soul's place. I could heap up words against you, and shake my head at you; but I would strengthen you with my mouth, and the comfort of my lips would relieve your grief. Job 16:2-5

Consider the advice Job received from his wife:

And he took for himself a potsherd with which to scrape himself while he sat in the midst of the ashes.

*Then his wife said to him, "Do you still hold to your
integrity? Curse God and die!"*

*But he said to her, "You speak as one of the foolish
women speaks. Shall we indeed accept good from God,
and shall we not accept adversity?"*

In all this Job did not sin with his lips. Job 2:8-10

One of the most difficult experiences a person faces
in the midst of suffering is to receive well-intentioned
counsel to give up the struggle. This counsel usually
comes from those who are closest to us and who love
us the most. It was Jesus' best friends who tried to talk
Him out of going to Jerusalem as we have seen with
Peter's rebuke. It was Job's own wife who told him,
"Curse God and die!" It was his wife who encouraged
him to compromise his integrity in order to alleviate
his pain.

She meant well. She obviously had compassion on
her husband. She encouraged him to take the easy way
out. Her words only served to increase Job's
frustration. Job did not understand why God had
called him to suffer but he did understand that God
had called him to suffer. It was hard enough for him to
be faithful to his vocation without his loved ones
trying to talk him out of it.

I remember vividly my first visit to the Crystal
Cathedral in Garden Grove, California. I was given a
tour of the grounds by one of Robert Schuller's
associate ministers. Our tour took us to a statue hewn
out of stone by a Scandinavian sculptor. It was a
sculpture of the figure of Job. I was overcome by
emotion as I stood before this majestic piece of art. It
displayed the figure of Job, his body twisted and
distorted in agony. The muscular detail was
reminiscent of a work by Michelangelo.

As I stared at the figure I thought of a technique employed by artists that followed the aesthetic principle articulated by the philosopher Herder. It is the principle of the "fruitful moment." Painters and sculptors, for example, do not ply their craft by the use of movie cameras or television recorders. Their objects are still, frozen in a single moment of time. The goal of the artist is to capture the crystallized essence of their subject by focusing on one fruitful or pregnant moment that tells the story. It was why Rembrandt sketched scores of scenes from the lives of biblical characters before he decided on a single frame to paint. It is Michelangelo's *David* reaching for a stone. It is Rodin's *Thinker* poised in deep reflection. It is the body of Christ cradled in the arms of His mother in the *Pieta*.

So the sculptor who fashioned the image of Job in the garden of the Crystal Cathedral, caught Job in the fruitful moment of the nadir of his agony. At the base of the sculpture, chiseled in the stone were these words: "Though He slay me, yet will I trust Him" (Job 13:15).

When I saw these words at the base of the statue I stood and wept in silence. No more heroic words were ever uttered by mortal man than these words of testimony from the lips of Job. "Though He slay me, yet will I trust Him."

God Himself as the Answer to "Why Am I Suffering?"

Job's trust wavered, but it never died. He mourned. He cried. He protested. He questioned. He even cursed the day of his birth. But he clutched tightly to his only

possible hope, his trust in God. At times Job was
hanging on by his fingernails. But he hung on. He
cursed himself. He rebuked his wife, but he never
cursed God.

Job cried out for God to answer his questions. He
desperately wanted to know why he was called upon
to endure so much suffering. Finally God answered
him out of the whirlwind. But the answer was not
what Job expected. God refused to grant Job a detailed
explanation of His reasons for the affliction. The
secret counsel of God was not disclosed to Job.

Ultimately the only answer God gave to Job was a
revelation of Himself. It was as if God said to him,
"Job, *I* am your answer." Job was not asked to trust a
plan but a Person, a personal God who is sovereign,
wise, and good. It was as if God said to Job, "Learn
who I am. When you know me, you know enough to
handle anything."

God was asking Job to exercise an implicit faith. An
implicit faith is not blind faith. It is a faith with vision,
a vision enlightened by a knowledge of the character
of God.

If God never revealed anything about Himself to us
and required that in this darkness we should trust
Him, indeed the requirement would be for blind faith.
We would be asked to make a blind leap of faith into
the awful abyss of darkness.

But God never requires such foolish leaps. He never
calls us to jump into the darkness. On the contrary, He
calls us to forsake the darkness, and enter into the
light. It is the light of His countenance. It is the radiant
light of His Person, which has no shadow of turning in
it. When we are bathed in the refulgent splendor of the
glory of His person then trust is not blind.

When Job declared, "Though He slay me, yet will I trust Him," he was revealing to us that though his knowledge of God was limited, it was still profound. He knew enough about the character of God to know that God is trustworthy. To be trustworthy simply means to be worthy of trust.

God deserves to be trusted. He merits our trust in Him. The more we understand of His perfections the more we understand how trustworthy He is. That is why the Christian pilgrimage is one that moves from faith to faith, from strength to strength, from grace to grace. It moves in a pattern of a rising crescendo. Ironically, it is through suffering and tribulation that the progress moves. That is why Paul could write these words:

We also glory in tribulations, knowing that tribulation produces perseverance; and perseverance, character; and character, hope. Now hope does not disappoint, because the love of God has been poured out in our hearts by the Holy Spirit who was given to us.
Romans 5:5

Here we are told that "hope does not disappoint." Other translations speak of a hope for which we are not ashamed or embarrassed.

Blind hope, like blind faith, will indeed disappoint us. Blind hope gropes aimlessly in the darkness. It stumbles over unseen obstacles. To put all one's hope into a single goal and to have that goal unfulfilled is to be disappointed.

Hope that is blind can be embarrassing. We stick our necks out only to be left in disgrace if our boldness does not pan out. The hope that rests in Christ will not be an embarrassment. The shame will be upon those who put their hope in something else. The hope that fails is the hope that has no power to overcome death.

If I hope in anything or anyone less than one who has power over death, I am doomed to final disappointment. Suffering will drive me to hopelessness. What character I have will disintegrate.

It is the hope of Christ that makes it possible for us to persevere in times of tribulation and distress. We have an anchor for our souls that rests in the One who has gone before us and conquered.

CHAPTER FOUR
DYING IN FAITH

The question that plagues us about death is not *if* we
will die. There is a macabre jocularity about the two
most certain things in life—death and taxes. But some
people do manage to avoid or evade taxes. The only
way we can possibly avoid death is to remain alive
until the return of Christ.

I just had to change the words of the last sentence.
At first I wrote these words: "The only way we can
possibly avoid death is to *be alive at* the return of
Christ." I changed the wording because my original
sentence was at least misleading and at worst heretical.
The New Testament assures us that those who are in

Christ will certainly be alive at His coming. If we die
before He returns we will be raised to witness His
glorious return:

But I do not want you to be ignorant, brethren,
concerning those who have fallen asleep lest you
sorrow as others who have no hope. For if we believe
that Jesus died and rose again, even so God will bring
with Him those who sleep in Jesus.

For this we say to you by the word of the Lord, that
we who are alive and remain until the coming of the
Lord will by no means precede those who are asleep.
For the Lord Himself will descend from heaven with a
shout, with the voice of an archangel, and with the
trumpet of God. And the dead in Christ will rise first.

Then we who are alive and remain shall be caught
up together with them in the clouds to meet the Lord
in the air. And thus we shall always be with the Lord.

Therefore comfort one another with these words.
1 Thessalonians 4:13-18

Here the Apostle Paul gives a vivid description of
what is popularly called the Rapture of the saints. No
Christian will miss the Rapture. Those who remain
alive until it happens will have no advantage over
those who have already died. The dead in Christ will
be raised for this event.

I remember as a child having to go to bed before the
Fourth of July fireworks display. I didn't want to go to
sleep for fear that I would miss all the fun. My parents
overcame my anxiety by promising me that they would
waken me in time to see the fireworks. They kept their
promise.

No Christian will sleep through the Second Coming of Christ. None of us are eyewitnesses to the birth of Christ. We missed His display of miracles during His earthly ministry. No one alive today beheld Christ on the cross. None of us are eyewitnesses of His glorious resurrection and ascension into heaven. But we will all be eyewitnesses of His return. The climax of the exaltation of Jesus will be viewed by every believer. God will raise the dead to make certain that every eye shall behold His triumphant return.

This event circumscribes the only "if" about our dying.

The Great Divide: Dying in Faith or in Sin

We have many questions about our own deaths. We wonder *where* we will die. We wonder *when* we will die. We ask *why* we will die. The chief concern of Scripture, however, is *how* we will die. This is the big question, the question that is loaded with significance.

I once received a note from my theological mentor, Dr. John Gerstner. In that note he passed on news to me of a mutual friend who had succumbed from cancer. Gerstner's simple but poignant words were these: "Tom Graham died in faith."

Those five words, "Tom Graham died in faith," said a lot to me. Gerstner was saying that Tom died as a Christian. Tom remained faithful to the end.

Scripture has much to say about *how* we die. From a biblical standpoint, there are only two possible ways of dying. Here the Bible passes over the various *causes* of death. We know that we can die of cancer, from a heart attack, from strangulation, from a gunshot wound, or from a host of other mortal causes. But these causes of biological death are not the chief concern of Scripture.

When the Scripture speaks of the *how* of death, the focus is on the spiritual state of the person at the time of his death. Here we see the "how" of death reduced to only two options. We either die in faith or we die in our sins.

Son of man, I have made you a watchman for the house of Israel; therefore hear a word from My mouth, and give them warning from Me: When I say to the wicked, "You shall surely die," and you give him no warning, nor speak to warn the wicked from his wicked way to save his life, that same wicked man shall die in his iniquity; but his blood I will require at your hand. Yet, if you warn the wicked, and he does not turn from his wickedness, nor from his wicked way, he shall die in his iniquity; but you have delivered your soul. Ezekiel 3:17-19

What Ezekiel declares in the Old Testament, Jesus reaffirms in the New Testament: "Therefore I said to you that you will die in your sins; for if you do not believe that I am He, you will die in your sins" (John 8:24).

We sometimes think that the worst thing that can befall a person is to die. That is not the message of Jesus. According to Christ, the worst possible thing that can befall us is to die in our sins.

This is the biblical message that is so widely ignored in our day. We like to believe that everyone who dies automatically goes to heaven. We assume that the only ticket required for entrance into the kingdom of God is death. The warning required by Ezekiel is ignored because we do not believe it is necessary.

The Need for Words of Warning

Recently I had the opportunity of speaking with Billy Graham. During our conversation I mentioned to him an experience I had as a college student. I recalled standing around a television set in the men's dormitory in the late fifties. Some of us had gathered to watch a television show on which Billy Graham was being interviewed.

When the host interviewed Billy Graham he tried to keep the interview light and humorous. He joked about the state of his own soul. Dr. Graham kept his poise and with dignity and grace told the host on national television that he needed Christ.

Thirty years later I asked Dr. Graham about that episode. He replied that he still keeps in touch with the host and reminds him of his need for Christ. Dr. Graham really cares about the man and does not want the talk show host to die in his sins.

Speaking to a dying person about the need for a Savior is not an easy matter. The last thing we want to do to a person in such a condition is to disturb him in any way or to make him feel uncomfortable. We think that it is an act of human kindness not to discuss such matters.

God commands us to speak to the dying about their need for a Savior. Ezekiel makes that crystal clear. If we love people we will warn them of the consequences of dying in their sins.

We remember the complaints that Jeremiah brought before God. Jeremiah was upset because God had called him to announce a warning to the people that they did not want to hear. To make matters worse for Jeremiah, his ministry was being undermined by false prophets who were very popular with the people because they told the people what they wanted to hear. They declared, "Peace, peace" when there was no peace. The Word of God declared

Do not listen to the words of the prophets who prophesy to you. They make you worthless; they speak a vision of their own heart, not from the mouth of the LORD. They continually say to those who despise Me, "The LORD has said, 'You shall have peace'"; and to everyone who walks according to the imagination of his own heart, "No evil shall come upon you."
Jeremiah 23:16-17

The message of the false prophets served only to "heal the hurt of the daughters of Zion, *slightly*." (See Jeremiah 8:10.) False words of comfort are like putting Band-Aids on cancer. The healing is at best slight. Here a crude form of slight temporary relief is substituted for the authentic balm of Gilead.

The great lie is the lie that declares there is no Last Judgment. Yet if Jesus of Nazareth taught anything, He emphatically declared that there would be a Last Judgment. We do not respect Jesus as a teacher if we ignore His teaching on this matter. Consider these words of Christ:

When the Son of Man comes in His glory, and all the holy angels with Him, then He will sit on the throne of His glory. All the nations will be gathered before Him,

*and He will separate them one from another, as a
shepherd divides his sheep from the goats. And He will
set the sheep on His right hand, but the goats on the
left. Then the King will say to those on His right hand,
"Come, you blessed of My Father, inherit the Kingdom
prepared for you from the foundation of the world."
. . . Then He will also say to those on the left hand,
"Depart from Me, you cursed, into the everlasting fire
prepared for the devil and his angels." . . . And these
will go away into everlasting punishment, but the
righteous into eternal life.* Matthew 25:31-46

Here Jesus utters sober words of warning. Those
who die in their sins will be separated; they will be
numbered with the goats.

Jesus amplifies this warning elsewhere. He warns
that "nothing is secret that will not be revealed, nor
anything hidden that will not be known and come to
light" (Luke 8:17). Again He says, "For there is
nothing covered that will not be revealed, nor hidden
that will not be known. Therefore, whatever you have
spoken in the dark will be heard in the light, and what
you have spoken in the ear in inner rooms will be
proclaimed on the housetops" (Luke 12:2-3).

Jesus warns that a day will come when all secrets
will become known. It will be the final end to all the
cover-ups of this world. Every closet will be open, and
the skeletons will be plainly visible. The sins of us all
will be made known unless we are "covered" by the
cloak of Christ's righteousness.

This future day of nakedness is a day when those
who die in their sins will "say to the mountains, 'Fall
on us!' and to the hills, 'Cover us!'" (Luke 23:30).

Fleeing the Wrath to Come

The New Testament describes Jesus as "Savior." The name "Jesus" was announced by the archangel Gabriel when he visited Mary. An angelic message to Joseph confirmed this name: "And she will bring forth a Son, and you shall call His name Jesus, for He will save His people from their sins" (Matthew 1:21).

The salvation of which the Bible speaks has a specific goal. The term *salvation* in general can be used for many things. Any type of rescue from danger or calamity can be called salvation. Biblically, a person can be saved from a disease or from financial disaster. If any army escapes defeat in battle it experiences salvation.

But the salvation wrought by Jesus is not of this general type. It is specific. Jesus saves us "from the wrath which is to come" (1 Thessalonians 1:10).

The preaching of John the Baptist accented this warning of the future. John spoke harshly to the Pharisees and Sadducees, the clergy of his day, saying, "Who has warned you to flee from the wrath to come?" (Matthew 3:7).

The warning that was given to first-century Israel is the same warning that is so woefully neglected in our own day.

Recently I overheard a conversation between two men. They were discussing the sermon preached by a guest minister in a Presbyterian church. The first asked, "How was the preacher on Sunday?"

The second man replied, "He was an old-fashioned preacher. He preached about fire and brimstone."

What qualified the preacher for being "old-fashioned" was that he preached on the Last Judgment. The concept is out of date. It is no longer in vogue. It is not fashionable to speak in our culture about final judgment.

I am sure that similar conversations were held in Jesus' day. Some who listened to the preaching of John the Baptist and of Jesus surely called them "old-fashioned." Perhaps the people said something like this: "Oh, those fellows are old-fashioned. They speak like the Old Testament prophets."

It is strange that we are so quick to dismiss as old-fashioned any mention of a final judgment. It is especially strange in a time and a culture that is so concerned about justice. We have worked for civil justice, for social justice, and for international justice. Yet we observe what the philosopher Immanuel Kant so acutely observed: justice does not always prevail in this world.

The God of Judeo-Christian history is a God of justice. His own character is just. For God not to correct injustices in this world, for God to let the scales of justice remain forever out of balance, would be for God to compromise His own integrity. This is precisely what He refuses to do. He promises ultimate justice.

Final Justice and Final Judgment

The Judge of all the earth cannot bring forth final justice without a final judgment. He insists that all human beings will be held accountable for their actions. If we are not ultimately accountable then the only conclusion we can reach is that ultimately we don't count. The bottom line would be that it doesn't matter ultimately how we live our lives. But every one of us knows that it does matter how people live. It matters to me how people treat me. It matters to you how people treat you.

Each one of us has been a victim at some point of injustice. Each one of us has committed injustices to other people. The reason we experience such injustice is because, as sinners, we are unjust people.

The dilemma we face is this: God is just. We are unjust. This is the worst dilemma a human being can face. For a guilty person to face the justice meted out in our criminal justice system is one thing. To stand before the tribunal of God is something else. We cry out with David, "If You, Lord, should mark iniquities, who could stand?" (Psalm 130:3).

David's question is a rhetorical question. The answer is obvious: *No one* will be able to stand. The central issue of Christianity is the issue of justification. It faces the dilemma squarely. The only possible way for an unjust person to stand in the presence of a just and holy God is to be justified. If we remain unjustified we die in our sins.

The only way we can be justified is by the righteousness of Christ. He alone has the merit necessary to cover us. That righteousness is received by faith. If we trust in Christ we are covered by His righteousness and are justified by faith. If we do not trust in Christ we will stand before God's judgment alone, an unjust person before a just God.

You may be thinking, "I am not an unjust person. I never murdered anybody. I never stole anything that was not mine." Indeed, if you are perfectly just you have no need of a Savior. If you've never broken the law of God, you have nothing to fear from His judgment.

We suffer, however, from two grand delusions. The

first delusion is that we are just enough to stand in the presence of God. It is a delusion because every one of us has sinned. We would be deluding ourselves in the extreme if we thought that we were perfect.

Only a few people become deluded enough to think that they are without sin. This is not the delusion most of us suffer. It is the second delusion that catches so many of us. The fact that God is just and that we are unjust doesn't seem to bother us. We nurture the hope that since God is also a loving and merciful God that He will make room for us in heaven even if we never repent of our sins and embrace Christ the Savior. We think that faith is not a necessary condition for salvation.

This delusion hurls an insult at the mercy of God. It assumes that by crucifying His only begotten Son for us, God did not do enough. That He requires faith and trust in the atoning Savior seems a bit narrow on His part.

The author of Hebrews labors the warning of the consequences that flow from ignoring the priestly act of atonement rendered by Jesus. He raises another rhetorical question: "How shall we escape if we neglect so great a salvation, which at the first began to be spoken by the Lord, and was confirmed to us by those who heard Him?" (Hebrews 2:3).

This danger of neglect is followed by further admonitions:

Beware, brethren, lest there be in any of you an evil heart of unbelief in departing from the living God; but exhort one another daily, while it is called "Today," lest any of you be hardened through the deceitfulness of sin. . . . And to whom did He swear that they

*would not enter His rest, but to those who did not
obey? So we see that they could not enter in because of
unbelief.* Hebrews 3:12-19

I don't know when it is that you are reading this
book. I have no way of knowing what the date is on
the calendar. But whatever day of the week or month
it is, one thing is certain: You are reading these words
"today." We notice that the admonition of Hebrews is
for today, while it is still today. If our neglect
continues until tomorrow, it may be too late.

The warning of Scripture stresses that as long as we
delay repentance and faith, we run the risk of being
"hardened" through the deceitfulness of sin. We've
heard the gospel preached so often that we can become
calloused to it. Our hearts become calcified; our
consciences seared. That is how sin works. First we
excuse ourselves and seek all manner of self-
justification. Finally we deceive ourselves into thinking
that faith and repentance are not necessary.

The Necessity of Not Delaying

God says that repentance and faith are necessary,
utterly necessary. Hebrews declares that God is so
serious about this that He swore a vow not to let the
disobedient enter into His rest. Never was a more
sacred oath sworn than this holy vow. It is the worst
kind of delusion to even entertain the possibility that
God might not keep this vow.

The author of Hebrews concludes by saying: "So we
see that they could not enter in because of unbelief"
(Hebrews 3:19).

If a person remains in unbelief it is simply not

possible for him to enter into the rest of God. Unbelief is a barrier to heaven.

We see then that there are only two ways of dying. We can die in faith, or we can die in our sins.

When will we face the judgment of God? Is there time for faith and repentance *after* we die?

Many people hold out hope for a second chance after death. The Roman Catholic church nurtures this hope with the doctrine of purgatory. Purgatory is a place of "purging" for those who need some cleansing before entering heaven. Therefore, masses are said and prayers are offered for the dead. (It is official Roman Catholic teaching that those in purgatory are baptized Christians who will, eventually, enter into heaven. However, it seems that in the popular imagination of many Catholics and others, purgatory is where sinners are given a second chance to mend their ways and make it to heaven, aided by the works of the living.)

If ever a doctrine was invented to meet the needs of a frightened humanity, it is the doctrine of purgatory. But Scripture offers not a shred of evidence to support the idea.

On the contrary, the urgent focus of Scripture is on the necessity of repentance *before* we die. Again it is the author of Hebrews who declares, "And as it is appointed for men to die once, but after this the judgment" (Hebrews 9:27).

I remember with much affection my uncle who lived in our house with us as we were growing up. He was a tough man with bulging muscles and a profane mouth. I vividly recall that he always seemed to have a solid black layer of grease visible under his fingernails. My uncle had no time for religion and church. He thought that religion was for sissies.

When I announced that I was going to seminary to prepare for the ministry, my uncle almost had an apoplexy. He teased me relentlessly. He joked that soon I'd be wearing my collar backward and would walk around in a black shirt.

Shortly after my ordination my uncle became terminally ill. About a week before he died I visited him in his room. He was dying and he knew it. Now there were no jokes. He was seriously concerned about where he was going. He said to me, "I'm not ready to go."

We talked about Christ. My uncle made a serious profession of faith. He got matters settled between himself and God. He died in faith.

Just as God swore an oath that the impenitent will not enter His rest, so He swore that those who repent and believe in Christ will enter His rest.

Again the author of Hebrews elaborates:

Therefore, since a promise remains of entering His rest, let us fear lest any of you seem to have come short of it. . . . For we who have believed do enter that rest. Hebrews 4:1-3

Hebrews concludes this fourth chapter with these words:

Seeing then that we have a great High Priest who has passed through the heavens, Jesus the Son of God, let us hold fast our confession. For we do not have a High Priest who cannot sympathize with our weaknesses, but was in all points tempted as we are, yet without sin. Let us therefore come boldly to the throne of grace, that we may obtain mercy and find grace to help in time of need. Hebrews 4:14-16

If we die in faith we join a great assembly of those who have gone before us. Hebrews provides a litany of the heroes of faith who have died.

By faith Abel offered to God a more excellent sacrifice. . . . By faith Enoch was translated. . . . By faith Noah, being divinely warned of things not yet seen, moved with godly fear, prepared an ark. . . . By faith Abraham obeyed when he was called to go out to the place which he would afterward receive as an inheritance. And he went out, not knowing where he was going. . . . By faith Sarah herself also received strength to conceive seed. . . . These all died in faith, not having received the promises, but having seen them afar off were assured of them, embraced them, and confessed that they were strangers and pilgrims on the earth. For those who say such things declare plainly that they seek a homeland. And truly if they had called to mind that country from which they had come out, they would have had opportunity to return. But now they desire a better, that is, a heavenly country. Therefore God is not ashamed to be called their God, for He has prepared a city for them. Hebrews 11:4-11, 13-16*

If we die in faith we will join Abel, Enoch, Noah, and the rest. We will be counted among those of whom God is not ashamed to be called their God. The city He has prepared will be ours. The just shall live by faith. They are indeed justified by faith, and the just shall die in faith.

CHAPTER FIVE
FAITH AND SUFFERING

The life of faith is not constant. Our faith wavers; it vacillates between moments of supreme exaltation and trying times that push us to the rim of despair. Doubt flashes danger lights at us and threatens our peace. Rare is the saint who has a tranquil spirit in all seasons.

Paul wrote poignantly about his own struggles in times of distress.

We are hard pressed on every side, yet not crushed; we are perplexed, but not in despair; persecuted, but not forsaken; struck down, but not destroyed—always

carrying about in the body the dying of the Lord Jesus,
that the life of Jesus also may be manifested in our
body. 2 Corinthians 4:8-10

We all know what it means to be hard pressed. We
use the word *pressure* to describe tense moments in
our lives. Trouble in the job, trouble in the marriage,
trouble in our relationships can mount up and attack
our spirit.

When we add the tragic death of a loved one or the
difficulty of a prolonged illness to these other daily
pressures, then we feel the pain of being hard pressed.

Paul says that we are "hard pressed on every side,
yet not crushed." Here the borders of our suffering are
defined. There is no attempt to mask pain in a
fraudulent piety. The Christian is not a Stoic. Neither
does he flee into a fantasy world that denies the reality
of suffering. Paul freely admitted the pressure he
experienced.

To be hard pressed is to feel like we are a used
automobile that has been consigned to the junk heap
and put in a metal compactor. To be hard pressed is to
feel a massive weight upon us, a pressing weight that
threatens to crush us.

When we experience severe heartbreak we may be
inclined to use the words, "I'm crushed." But this is
hyperbole. We may feel crushed; we may even come
close to being crushed. But the bold declaration of the
apostle is that we are *not* crushed.

We speak of "the straw that breaks the camel's
back." We amplify the expression by speaking of the
"last straw."

Recently I joined Weight Watchers. At the initial
meeting for orientation everyone was given several
items including a food guide, a daily chart for

recording what was consumed, an exercise booklet, and a drinking straw. As we neared the end of the meeting and the instructions for the program were completed, the instructor asked, "What made you decide to join Weight Watchers?" Several members of the group volunteered answers. Each person had a different reason. They saw themselves in a recent photograph and couldn't stand it; they had to increase a clothes size; they were told by their doctor to lose weight; and other reasons.

After this discussion the instructor held up a drinking straw. "This is your last straw," she said. "This straw represents the reason you decided to join the program. Take it home and put it in a prominent position. Tape it to the refrigerator. When you falter in your desire to lose weight, look at it. Let it serve to remind you of why you are here."

I doubt if a camel's back has ever been broken by a drinking straw. The original metaphor had its origin in the Middle East, where camels are still used as beasts of burden. The camel is expected to carry straw that is harvested. There is a limit to how much straw a camel can carry. Every camel's back has a breaking point. The difference between a tolerable burden and one that crushes may be a single piece of straw.

I don't know how much straw a camel can carry. I don't know how heavy a burden I can carry. We all have a tendency, however, to suppose that we can carry far less than we actually can.

"My Burden Is Light"

There have been times in my life when I have uttered foolish prayers. When I have been hard pressed I have cried out to God, "This much and no more, Lord. I can't handle another setback. One more straw and I'm finished." It seems that every time I pray like that God puts a fresh load on my back. It is as if He answers my prayer by saying, "Don't tell Me how much you can bear."

God knows our limits far better than we do. In one respect we are very much like camels. When the camel's load is already heavy he doesn't ask his master for more weight. His knees get a bit wobbly, and he groans beneath the burden, but there is still room for more before his back will break.

The promise of God is not that He will never give us more weight to carry than we want to carry. The promise of God is that he will never put more upon us than we can actually bear.

Note that Paul did not say, "We are easy pressed on every side." He said that we are hard pressed. At first glance these words seem in direct conflict with the promises of Christ. Jesus said,

Come to Me, all you who labor and are heavy laden, and I will give you rest. Take My yoke upon you and learn from Me, for I am gentle and lowly in heart, and you will find rest for your souls. For My yoke is easy and My burden is light. Matthew 11:28-30

It is this last sentence that has made me wonder. It does not always seem to me that the burden Christ gives us is so light. It almost seems as if Jesus approaches us under false pretenses. But His words are true. He does give rest to those who are heavy laden. The terms *easy* and *light* are relative terms. Easy is relative to a standard of difficulty. Light is relative to a standard of heaviness. What is difficult to bear without Christ is made far more bearable with Christ. What is a heavy burden to carry alone becomes a far lighter burden to carry with His help.

It is precisely the presence and help of Christ in times of suffering that makes it possible for us to stand up under pressure. It is because of Christ that Paul could triumphantly declare that though he was hard pressed, he was not crushed. We may feel like an automobile in a metal compactor, but Christ stands as a shield for us to prevent the weight from falling upon us entirely.

To suffer without Christ is to risk being totally and completely crushed. I've often wondered how people cope with the trials of life without the strength found in Christ. His presence and comfort are so vital that I'm not surprised when unbelievers accuse Christians of using religion as a crutch. We remember Karl Marx's charge that religion is the opium of the masses. He was referring to opiate as a narcotic used for dulling the effects of pain. Others have charged that religion is a bromide used by the weak in times of trouble.

Several years ago I had knee surgery. During my recuperation I used crutches. I used the crutches because I needed them. Likewise, years earlier I was in the hospital for another operation. After surgery I was given painkilling drugs every four hours. I recall watching the clock during the fourth hour, eagerly awaiting the moment when I could push the call button for the nurse to get another dose. I was grateful for the painkiller. I was grateful for my crutches.

I am even more grateful for Christ. It is no shame to call upon His help in times of trouble. It is His delight to minister to us in our time of pain. There is no scandal in the mercy of God to the afflicted. He is like a Father who pities His children and moves to comfort them in times of pain. To suffer without the comfort of God is no virtue. To lean upon His comfort is no vice, contrary to Karl Marx.

Paul adds, "We are perplexed, but not in despair." Perplexity often accompanies suffering. When we are stricken with illness or grief we are often bewildered and confused. Our first question is why. We ask, How could God allow this to happen to me?

I remember the story of a distraught father who was deeply grieved by the death of his son. He went to see his pastor and in bewildered anger said, "Where was God when my son died?" The pastor replied with a calm spirit, "The same place He was when His Son died."

Surprised by Suffering

There is an element of surprise connected to suffering. We learn early that pain is a part of life, but the learning process is usually gradual. I am amused by the way my three-year-old grandson handles pain. When something hurts him he declares, "Pap-pap, I have an 'ouch.'" He used the exclamation "ouch" as a noun. If the "ouch" is slight, a simple kiss will make it disappear. If it is more severe he asks for an "andbaid."

Most childhood illnesses and bruises are minor. When a child gets a stomach virus he usually doesn't worry about cancer. He learns quickly that the discomfort of childhood diseases is soon over. It is as adults that we move into another level of disease and pain. Though we move through stages of preparation, we are never quite ready when we are afflicted with more serious illnesses.

I remember my daughter's first visit to the hospital. She was six years old and had to have her tonsils removed. As parents we went through all the steps of both preparing her and shielding her from what was coming. We read the children's books together about going to the hospital. We assured her that after the operation she would be allowed the treat of her favorite ice cream.

The trip to the hospital was an adventure. The pediatric wing of the hospital was gaily decorated. The nurses entertained our daughter and her roommate with toys. Her spirits were high and apprehension was at a minimum.

When the girls were taken into surgery we awaited their return from the recovery room. I will never forget the vision of my daughter when she looked at me after she had awakened. She was a pitiful sight. Dried blood was crusted at the edge of her lips. Her face was ashen. But what was most haunting was the look of fear, shock, and betrayal. She was experiencing a new threshold of pain. It was as if she were saying to me with her eyes, "How could you? You knew it would be like this and you lied to me." The last thing she cared about at that moment was ice cream.

My daughter was surprised by the pain. She was perplexed. Her pain was not what she expected. I am sure she had the same questions about me as we do about our heavenly Father when sudden pain is thrust upon us.

When perplexity is added to suffering we sense a surprise that God has allowed such deep affliction to befall us. The surprise stems not so much from what

God leads us to believe but from what we hear from misguided teachers. The zealous person who promises us a life free from suffering has found his message from some other source than Scripture.

We are admonished by Scripture not to think that it is a strange or unusual thing that we should suffer. Peter wrote,

Beloved, do not think it strange concerning the fiery trial which is to try you, as though some strange thing has happened to you, but rejoice to the extent that you partake of Christ's sufferings, that when His glory is revealed, you may also be glad with exceeding joy.
1 Peter 4:12-13

Here Peter echoes the theme we have already noted in the writings of Paul. Where Paul spoke of "filling up that which is lacking" in the sufferings of Christ, Peter speaks of "partaking" of Christ's sufferings.

Peter adds these words:

But let none of you suffer as a murderer, a thief, an evildoer, or as a busybody in other people's matters. Yet if anyone suffers as a Christian, let him not be ashamed, but let him glorify God in this matter.
1 Peter 4:15-16

When the criminal suffers for his crime, he may be distressed, but he has no reason to be perplexed. There is no surprise that punishment should be the consequence of crime. There is shame attached to this sort of suffering.

To suffer as a Christian carries no shame. Peter concludes:

Therefore let those who suffer according to the will of God commit their souls to Him in doing good, as to a faithful Creator. 1 Peter 4:19

In this conclusion Peter erases all doubt about the question of whether it is ever the will of God that we should suffer. He speaks of those who suffer "according to the will of God." This text means that suffering itself is part of the sovereign will of God.

Earlier in his epistle Peter had spoken of the fruit of our suffering:

In this you greatly rejoice, though now for a little while, if need be, you have been grieved by various trials, that the genuineness of your faith, being much more precious than gold that perishes, though it is tested by fire, may be found to praise, honor, and glory at the revelation of Jesus Christ, whom having not seen you love. Though now you do not see Him, yet believing, you rejoice with joy inexpressible and full of glory, receiving the end of your faith—the salvation of your souls. 1 Peter 1:6-9

This passage reveals the answer to how it is possible to be perplexed, but not in despair. Our suffering has a purpose. It has a goal—the end of our faith is the salvation of our souls. Suffering is a crucible. As gold is refined in the fire, purged of its dross and impurities, so is our faith tested by fire. Gold perishes. Our souls do not. We experience pain and grief for a season. It is while we are in the fire that perplexity assails us. But there is another side to the fire. As the dross burns away, the genuineness of faith is purified unto the salvation of our souls.

Despair and the Desire to Die

It is when we view our suffering as meaningless—
without purpose—that we are tempted to despair. A
woman who endures the travail of childbirth is able to
do it because she knows that the end result will be a
new life.

Those who are terminally ill do not have the same
hope of a good result as in childbearing. Here the pain
appears to be unto death rather than unto life. Indeed
that would be true if there is no salvation. If death is
the end then the suffering that attends it would drive
us to full and final despair. The message of Christ is
that death is not unto death but unto life. The analogy
of childbirth applies. It is used to describe the suffering
of Christ and of the whole creation: "He shall see the
travail of his soul and be satisfied" (Isaiah 53:11).

*For we know that the whole creation groans and
labors with birth pangs together until now. And not
only they, but we also who have the first fruits of the
Spirit, even we ourselves groan within ourselves,
eagerly waiting for the adoption, the redemption of
our body.* Romans 8:22-23

We are perplexed, but not in despair. The pain of
suffering in itself is enough to drive us to despair were
we not persuaded of the redemption that lies before us.
Even that redemption, however, is not always enough
to keep us from approaching the rim of despair.

Scripture repeatedly reveals the struggles of the
greatest saints with the problem of despair. More than
one biblical figure cursed the day of his birth and
pleaded for the privilege of death. Moses faced the
dark night of the soul when he cried out to God,

*If You treat me like this, please kill me here and now—
if I have found favor in Your sight—and do not let me
see my wretchedness!* Numbers 11:15

Job cursed the day of his birth, saying,

*Why did I not die at birth? Why did I not perish when
I came from the womb? Why did the knees receive
me? Or why the breasts, that I should nurse? For now
I would have lain still and been quiet, I would have
been asleep; then I would have been at rest.*
Job 3:11-13

Jeremiah expressed the same sentiment.

*Cursed be the day in which I was born! Let the day
not be blessed in which my mother bore me! Let the
man be cursed who brought news to my father, saying,
"A male child has been born to you!" making him very
glad. . . . Why did I come forth from the womb to see
labor and sorrow, that my days should be consumed
with shame?* Jeremiah 20:14-15, 18

The Danish philosopher Søren Kierkegaard once
remarked that one of the worst states a human being
can face is to want to die and not be allowed to die.
Many elderly people have said to me, "I wish the Lord
would take me. Why does He make me linger?"

The deep desire to be released from suffering lies at
the core of the issue of euthanasia. The lethal injection
is seen as a kind of mercy-killing. It is argued that we
are more humane to animals than we are to people. We
shoot horses. We put our dogs to sleep.

God does not permit us to commit suicide. Suicide,

in its fullest expression, involves a surrender to despair. (This does *not* mean that suicide is the unpardonable sin. People commit suicide for all sorts of reasons and in all sorts of conditions. We don't really know the state of mind people are in when they do it. We leave the question of the fate of suicide victims to the mercy of God.) Whatever the complexities of suicide involve in the judgment of God, we know that we are not given suicide as a proper option for death.

Death with Dignity?

The issue of euthanasia is also complex. Distinctions are made between *active* and *passive* euthanasia. Active euthanasia involves taking direct steps to kill a suffering person. Simply stated, passive euthanasia involves the cessation of the use of extraordinary life support methods.

Modern technology has introduced severe moral dilemmas into the matter of dying. Historically, both the church and the medical profession (following the Hippocratic Oath) have followed the maxim that we ought to do everything possible to sustain life. With the advent of modern techniques it is now possible to keep people technically alive beyond the scope of any possible human hope for recovery.

Here the issue of dying with dignity becomes paramount. Excruciating questions are often faced: *Who pulls the plug?* and *When may the plug be pulled?*

I was recently asked to address a medical convocation of eight hundred physicians on the issue of "pulling the plug." The issue was not focused on active euthanasia but on the question of *allowing nature to take its course.* The doctors were acutely aware of the problems. There are many ways to "pull the plug." IV tubes can be removed, allowing a person to starve to death. Respirators can be turned off. Medication can be stopped.

When we consider the various means by which life can be artificially sustained or terminated, the line between so-called active and passive euthanasia quickly becomes blurred. Likewise the difference between *ordinary* and *extraordinary* means of life support is not always clear. Yesterday's extraordinary means becomes today's ordinary means.

The problem is complicated by the question of *who* makes the decision. The doctor doesn't want to play God. The family can be crushed by guilt surrounding the decision. The clergy doesn't feel adequate to the task, and it is terrifying to leave the issue in the hands of the legal community.

Yet decisions in these matters are required to be made daily in hospitals all over the world. Not to make a decision is to make a decision.

I don't have all the answers to this dilemma. Two things I'm sure of. The first is that the issues must be decided in light of the overarching principle of the sanctity of human life. We must bend over backwards to insure the maintenance of human life. If we err it is better to err in favor of life rather than to cheapen it in any way. Secondly, the decision must involve three parties at least, perhaps four. It must involve the consultation of the physicians, the family, the clergy, and when possible, the patient.

This issue is part of the perplexity of suffering. At all costs the decisions we make must not be made from a point of view of despair. At all times we must keep the goal of redemption in mind lest hope is swallowed up by despair.

David summed up the matter:

I would have lost heart, unless I had believed that I would see the goodness of the LORD in the land of the living. Psalm 27:13

In the same epistle in which the Apostle Paul said, "We are perplexed, but not in despair," he gave voice to his own struggle at the rim of despair:

For we do not want you to be ignorant, brethren, of our trouble which came to us in Asia; that we were burdened beyond measure, above strength, so that we despaired even of life. Yes, we had the sentence of death in ourselves, that we should not trust in ourselves but in God who raised the dead, who delivers us from so great a death, and does deliver us; in whom we trust that He will still deliver us.
2 Corinthians 1:8-10

Paul entered into despair. But his despair was limited. It was not ultimate despair. He despaired of his earthly life. He was sure that he was going to die. But Paul did not despair of the ultimate deliverance from death. He knew the promise of Christ for victory over death.

Herein is the crisis of faith. Is death final? Or is there something beyond the grave that makes all the suffering we are called to endure worthwhile?

The rest of this book will focus on two major concerns. The first is, *Is there really a heaven?* The second is, *What is heaven like?*

PART TWO

Life After Death

CHAPTER SIX
THE POPULAR VIEW OF LIFE AFTER DEATH

Not long ago I visited with my aunt who was born in the year 1900. It was a time of reminiscence, of nostalgia. I queried her with all of my questions of roots, family history, and the rattling of old skeletons from old closets.

She leaned back in her rocking chair and spoke with misty eyes of the old days. She filled in the gaps about my father's life and my grandparents' lives. The highlight of this excursion in time was her recollections of my great-grandfather.

Great-grandfather's name was Charles Sproul. (Hence the origin of the "C" in my own name, R. C.)

Charles Sproul was born in County Donegal, Ireland, in 1824. He arrived in this country in 1843 with no shoes on his feet, having left a thatched roof cottage with a mud floor in the old country. During the Civil War he was Fireman Third Class aboard the U.S.S. *Grampus* in the Union Navy. He fought at the Battle of Vicksburg. He died in 1910 at the age of eighty-six.

This conversation with my aunt took place in the summer of 1987, 163 years after my great-grandfather was born. When Charles Sproul died he had been living at the home of my grandfather in Pittsburgh. My aunt knew him for ten years before he died.

It was a spooky feeling to be talking to someone who had vivid memories of a person who was born in 1824. So much time, so much history has transpired since that date. I wondered what it would be like if I lived to be eighty-six and could tell my great-grandchildren the stories I heard, first person, from someone who knew my own great-grandfather. I will be eighty-six in the year 2025. That would span a time frame of over two centuries.

When Charles Sproul was born, the United States was only a few decades old. James Monroe was president of the United States. No one had heard of Abraham Lincoln. There was no transcontinental railroad, no automobiles, no airplanes, radios, televisions, not even an electric light bulb.

Charles Sproul is gone. This world has changed. I don't even know where Charles Sproul is buried. His son, Robert, married a girl who had traveled from Ohio, up the Ohio River, to Pittsburgh by steamboat. Robert died in 1945. His sons both died in 1956.

My son was born in 1965. His name is Robert, but

he goes by R. C. He is the last surviving Sproul from our family. Perhaps he will have a son someday. If not, the family name will perish with him.

The Bible says that "all flesh is grass." It grows—it withers—it dies.

Recently a man asked me about my long-term goals. He said, "What do you want to be doing with your life in five years? In ten years?" Five or ten years hardly seems like a long term for me. To a teenager they seem like an eternity.

A more relevant question for me is, What will I be doing one hundred years from now? It may seem like a silly question. It sounds almost like the question, What was I doing one hundred years ago?

One hundred years ago I didn't exist. My sister didn't exist. My dear old aunt didn't exist. My father didn't exist. Old Charles Sproul did exist, and so did his son, Robert. But they are gone, as I will also be gone.

Few if any people who read this book will have been alive one hundred years ago. Almost certainly no one who reads this book will be alive one hundred years from now.

Or will they? Do we have a future that will last one hundred years from now and beyond?

The Quest for Knowledge of the Future

I am amused when I pass little houses or storefronts that advertise palm readers. Often they are adorned with a silhouette of a human hand. The billboard promises: Know Your Future. Fortunes are told with tarot cards, crystal balls, and above all by reading the secrets found in the palm of your hand.

It always amazes me that the establishments of palm readers seem to have a run-down look to them. Business must be bad. It seems a shame that the art of palmistry somehow never seems to penetrate the vagaries of the stock market.

Doris Day once had a smash hit with the popular song, "Que Será, Será, What Will Be, Will Be." The words went something like this:

When I was just a little girl, I asked my mother, What will I be? Will I be pretty? Will I be rich? What will my future be?

The mother's answer was vague. She had no crystal ball. All she could offer in response was the refrain, *Que será, será*—What will be, will be.

We worry about the future precisely because we do not know what it holds for us. The only reliable source for absolute knowledge of the future comes from the Lord of the Future. Where God speaks of the future we have sound reason for hope. Where He is silent we are to desist from inquiry. The Old Testament abounds with severe prohibitions coupled with severe penalties for those who seek to see beyond the veil of time by illegitimate means.

But the ultimate question of our future plagues every human soul. Job asked the question this way: "If a man dies, will he live again?" (Job 14:14).

Since death intruded into Paradise, the question of life after the grave has been paramount. Virtually every human culture has developed some form of hope in life beyond the grave. The ancient Egyptians placed precious items in the tombs of their deceased loved ones in hope that these items would be useful in the afterlife. The American Indians had their concept of a happy hunting ground, the Norse had their hopes of Valhalla. The Jews had their shadowy concept of Sheol, the Greeks their view of Hades in the Stygian darkness.

Eastern religion counters well with a view of reincarnation made popular by Shirley MacLaine and others in this country. The Bridey Murphy episode of American parapsychology added to the speculation of multiple incarnations. As far back as Plato we have seen men argue for some theory of reincarnation.

The Greek Arguments for Life After Death

In the ancient world, Plato (428-348 B.C.) came under the influence of a group of philosophers called the Pythagoreans. The Pythagoreans are famous for the mystical significance they attached to numbers. The founder of the school, Pythagoras, developed the now famous Pythagorean theorem that occupies a place in modern geometry. The Pythagoreans also conceived of the idea of the "transmigration of the soul," or reincarnation.

Their theory rested on the Greek premise that the human soul is immortal and eternal. The soul pre-exists the body. When a human person is born, an eternal soul is temporarily "trapped" within a body. The body is a kind of prison house for the soul. The physical body, or prison, undergoes the process of generation and decay. The outward body finally dies, and the soul is released from its prison. In various views of reincarnation the soul is then incarnated once more in a new body. The soul migrates. It might be reincarnated in a higher form of life or a lower one.

Usually the various migrations or incarnations are dictated by the level of virtue achieved in the most recent incarnation. Ultimate redemption occurs when the soul finally breaks free of the body and continues as a disembodied spirit, free of the inhibiting influence of the physical body. Plato basically accepted these premises, adding further insights of his own.

THE ANALOGY FROM NATURE

Plato set forth his speculations about life after death in his famous *Phaedo* dialogue. The scene takes place in an Athenian prison cell, where Socrates awaits execution for his "crime" of corrupting the youth of Athens by his penetrating and disturbing philosophical inquiries. We meet Socrates in his final hours as he awaits the visit of the guard who will soon bring him a fatal draught of hemlock. Socrates is surrounded by his friends and students. (Plato is absent because of illness.) There is a stark contrast in mood between the cheery disposition of Socrates and the frightened apprehension of his friends, who have already entered into mourning.

Socrates spends his final hours teaching his students about the anticipated joys of life after death. Socrates says to his friends,

My words, too, are only an echo; but there is no reason why I should not repeat what I have heard: and indeed, as I am going to another place, it is very meet for me to be thinking and talking of the nature of the pilgrimage which I am about to make. What can I do better in the interval between this and the setting of the sun?[1]

1. *The Works of Plato*, ed. Irwin Edman (New York: Random House, 1956), 114.

Socrates declares his confidence in a future life by initiating a lengthy discussion on the theme:

And now, O my judges, I desire to prove to you that the real philosopher has reason to be of good cheer when he is about to die, and that after death he may hope to obtain the greatest good in the other world.[2]

What follows is an elaborate and complex "proof" for the immortality of the soul. Socrates gives an *argument from opposites.* He speculates about a universal opposition of all things—that there is a process that we observe daily in nature by which things are generated by their opposites. Sleep proceeds to wakefulness, which in turn proceeds inexorably to sleep. Something which becomes greater can only become greater after first being less. And that which undergoes diminution (becoming less) can only do so after first being greater.

In like manner, only that which is first alive can ever die. Life produces its opposite—death. So also death must produce its opposite, which is life.

THE THEORY OF RECOLLECTION

Socrates then attempts to prove that the souls of people existed before they were born. This argument rests on Plato's famous *theory of recollection.* In the recollection theory, Plato sought to prove (in this and other dialogues, especially in *Meno*) that we are born with certain ideas in our mind that can only come from a preexistent state of the soul. Our ideas of beauty, goodness, justice, and holiness, for example, are not acquired from experience in this life but are

2. Ibid., 117.

already present at birth. The whole process we call "learning" is, in reality, merely a kind of stimulation of the memory to recall those ideas we understood more clearly in our souls before the negative influence of bodily passions dimmed them at birth.

Once Socrates proves this idea of recollection, and with it the preexistence of the soul, it is an easy step to presume the continuing existence of the soul after the body dies.

One of Socrates' students, Cebes, remains skeptical. He says to his mentor,

Then, Socrates, you must argue us out of our fears— and yet, strictly speaking, they are not our fears, but there is a child within us to whom death is a sort of hobgoblin: him too we must persuade not to be afraid when he is alone in the dark.[3]

Socrates proceeds to argue that the soul is a spiritual essence. As a spiritual essence the soul is not made of matter, which is capable of decay or dissolution. It is by its very essence commutable. In a word, *it cannot die.* Here is Socrates' reply:

Then reflect, Cebes: of all which has been said is not this the conclusion?—that the soul is in the very likeness of the divine, and immortal, and intellectual, and uniform, and indissoluble, and unchangeable; and that the body is in the very likeness of the human, and the mortal, and unintellectual, and multiform, and dissoluble, and changeable. Can this, my dear Cebes, be denied?[4]

3. Ibid., 137.
4. Ibid., 140.

But there is a glitch in Socrates' reasoning. After he labors the point that the soul is unchangeable, he proceeds to declare that the soul is indeed changeable at one point. It is capable of moral corruption. He speaks of the pollution of the soul that must be cleansed through further incarnations.

What I mean is that men who have followed after gluttony, and wantonness, and drunkenness, and have had no thought of avoiding them, would pass into asses and animals of that sort.[5]

Socrates' speculation about reincarnation sounds a bit amusing to the modern reader (Shirley MacLaine notwithstanding). He speaks of men becoming wolves or hawks or bees or wasps. (It would seem that we ought to be a bit solicitous toward garden spiders lest we trample upon our great-great-grandfathers.)

The modern revival of interest in reincarnation raises some fascinating questions. Why, for example, do so many people find the idea of reincarnation so appealing?

A simple answer may be that reincarnation offers us a second chance at life. We tend to wonder how things would be if we had the opportunity to live our lives over again. We wonder what changes we would make. Our dreams are tormented by the "what ifs" and the "might have beens" of life.

We all carry a certain burden of unresolved guilt. A second trip through life offers the opportunity to atone for our sins, to make up for the failures and deficiencies of this life. The idea of repeated incarnations carries the hope of progress, the hope of

5. Ibid., 143.

rising higher and higher in our aspirations or our moral performance.

Yet reincarnation faces a massive difficulty that is rarely discussed among those who cling to the belief. It is the problem of continuity of conscious awareness.

I am a conscious human being. That consciousness includes a wonderful thing called memory. I remember experiences I had as a child. My memory bank stores a kind of knowledge of my own personal history. Of course, some of these memories are unpleasant, while others are delightful. I am my personal history. I am not simply what I happen to do, think, or feel at this moment. I am the same human personality that opened toys on Christmas morning in 1943. Certainly there have been changes in my body, my thinking, my *self* since 1943. These changes continue as life continues. But there is a continuity of personality from the child of 1943 to the adult of the present.

Now suppose that this life is my third or fourth or hundredth incarnation. How much do I remember of my previous incarnations? In my case, the answer is simple: nothing. I have absolutely no recollection of any life experience prior to my birth. I realize that some people have tried to prove via hypnosis and other measures that they do possess some deeply buried vague memory of a previous life. The arguments for this appear to indicate more of what we call imagination than of genuine memory.

Let me ask the reader: Do you remember living in this world before you were born? If not, then the dilemma is clear. Of what possible value is reincarnation if there is no conscious link between lives? If there is no continuity of consciousness, no memory whatever, how can we speak of personal continuity?

If I continue to live after this life with no link of personal consciousness, will what follows really be me?

This entire speculation, which may seem bizarre to us, is rooted in a profoundly important matter. Beneath the level of the argument lurks the problem of the polluted soul and the question of unsolved justice.

There is a concern among sensitive people that this world does not always carry out perfect justice. We all observe that too often the righteous suffer and the wicked prosper. The world is long on tooth, fang, and claw, and, contrary to Hollywood, Rocky loses more often than he wins.

The haunting question abides: Why should I engage in acts of charity and sacrifice if life does not guarantee justice? Indeed, the whole question of ethical conduct becomes a quagmire of uncertainty. Russian novelist Dostoevsky once remarked, "If there is no God, all things are permissible." Here he put his finger on the central issue: If there is no God, there is no guarantee of ultimate justice. If there is no guarantee of ultimate justice, why should anyone ever act out of moral obligation? Why not just act out of pure self-interest?

The Need for an "Ought" in the World

In our daily lives we cannot speak for very long without using words like *ought, should,* and *must.* We tell our children, "You ought to tell the truth." They may reply, "Why?" What do we say? We can rely on pure power tactics by replying, "Because I say so." We might appeal to their own self-interest by saying, "Because honesty is the best policy." But even a child wonders if honesty is the best policy if he has just confessed to stealing cookies out of the cookie jar.

Anytime someone says, "You ought" we might be tempted to respond with one of two common questions: "Sez who?" or "Why should I?"

These questions raise the issue of the basis or ground of moral obligation. Is there any real compelling reason why anyone can ever say "ought" about anything?

Our language reflects a crucial difference between two sentences. Sentence 1 reads:

"I *want* to do something."

Sentence 2 reads:

"I *ought* to do something."

The difference between these two sentences is the difference between *desire* and *duty*. If I desire to do what my duty requires, there is no conflict. If I want to do what I ought to do, my decisions are easy. Moral struggle enters the picture when there is a conflict between desire and duty. It is when I want to do what I ought not to do or I do not want to do what I ought to do that I feel the pangs of a disturbed conscience.

The term *ought* is used more than one way. German philosopher Immanuel Kant made a distinction between two types of oughtness or imperatives. He distinguished between a *hypothetical imperative* and a *moral imperative*.

A hypothetical imperative refers to a kind of oughtness that involves following certain means that are necessary to achieve certain desired ends. For example, if we go to work on a day that promises showers, we may say to ourselves: I *ought* to take my umbrella. Here we are not speaking about a moral duty. (Unless, of course, we imply a moral obligation to take care of our bodies.) Rather, what is in view is this: If I want to stay dry I must avail myself of the necessary means to achieve that end. I must have an umbrella to shield myself from the rain. If I want to stay dry, then I must carry my umbrella.

Consider another illustration. Suppose a person decides to become a burglar. He desires to become a successful burglar. He reasons like this: If I want to be a successful burglar, I ought to take precautions to make sure that I am not caught in the act of burglaring. Here the burglar is thinking in terms of a hypothetical imperative. If he were thinking in terms of a moral imperative he would be saying to himself, I ought not to be doing this burglary at all.

As soon as we move from the hypothetical to the moral, we enter the arena of duty. Duty involves the matter of ethics. Here the word *ought* indicates a moral obligation. It means that what I want to do must be subordinated to what I ought to do.

We all experience the conflict between desire and duty. We all know that there are things we desire to do that are not right. At least we feel the weight of such conflict. But suppose there is no such thing as a morally right thing to do. Suppose that right and wrong are mere social conventions, arbitrary rules that help society run smoothly. Suppose that all imperatives are merely hypothetical imperatives that never pass over into moral imperatives. Then all that matters is that burglars protect themselves from being caught. The only evil a burglar can do is to fail in his attempt to pull off a successful burglary.

What does all this have to do with life after death?

Everything. If there is no such thing as right and wrong, if there is no such thing as *moral* obligation, then there is no such thing as justness. If there is no such thing as justness, then ultimately there is no such thing as justice. Justice becomes a mere sentiment. It means the preferences of an individual or a group. If the majority in one society prefers that adultery be rewarded, then justice is served when an adulterer receives a prize for his adultery. If the majority in a different society prefers that adultery be punished, then justice is served if the adulterer is penalized. But in this schema there is no such thing as ultimate justice because the will of an individual or of a group can never serve as an ultimate moral norm for justice. It can reveal only a preference.

On the other hand, if there is such a thing as right and wrong we can talk about real justness. Then justice can be defined in terms of rewards and punishments distributed according to what is just. Then the term *ought* is packed with the power of real moral imperative.

What Kant and Dostoevsky wrestled with is this: Without ultimate justice, can there ever be a sound basis for moral duty? If there is no ultimate justice, then why be concerned with being just? If we push this a bit we can say that if my moral decisions do not count then *I* do not count. If my actions do not count ultimately, then my life does not count ultimately.

That is why Kant saw that life without moral obligation is life without meaning. Oh, to be sure, we can *assign* meaning to our lives based on personal preference and sentiment. But that is all we have, a sentimental wish that our lives have meaning. It is a sentimental wish that has both feet firmly planted in midair.

Kant recognized the universal reality of man's sense of right and wrong. Everyone functions with some sense of moral duty. We all feel the weight of the "I ought," of the imperative. Kant then asked the practical question, "What is practically necessary for this moral sense to be meaningful?"

His first conclusion was crucial. He argued that for the moral sense of duty to be meaningful there must be such a thing as justness. For justness, or right and wrong, to be meaningful, there must be justice. Thus justice serves as a necessary condition for moral obligation to be meaningful.

Ah, but here's the rub: In this world we recognize that justice is not always done. Too many burglars are successful in their burglaring. Does this mean that crime ultimately does pay and that there is no vindication for the just person?

That is the only conclusion we could reach if in fact there were no ultimate justice. There may be *proximate justice*, that is, partial and occasional justice where the burglar is caught and his victims' possessions are returned intact, but still the scales of justice would too often be out of balance. For justness to be meaningful ultimately, then we need more than proximate justice; we need ultimate justice.

If ultimate justice is to be had, then the first requirement that must be met is this: We must survive the grave. If we do not survive the grave, and if justice is not served perfectly in this world, then justice is not ultimate and our sense of moral obligation is a meaningless striving after the wind.

If ultimate justice is served then we must be there to experience it. Unless we survive the grave we cannot have justice. Here Kant is echoing the thoughts of Socrates and Plato, in addition to the thoughts of Job and Ecclesiastes.

The Need for the Perfect Judge

But suppose we do survive the grave. Suppose we
return in another incarnation as a wasp or a donkey.
We may still be haunted by further injustice. Like
Balaam's ass, we might have a master who beats us
without just cause. Or we might fly as a wasp into
some unjust fellow's burst of Raid.

We cannot have a trial without a person who is
being tried. But neither can there be a trial if the only
person present is the accused. There must be a judge.
No judge, no judgment. No judgment, no justice.

Therefore a second necessary condition for ultimate
justice is the presence of an ultimate judge. But this is
no ordinary judge that is required. For ultimate justice
to be insured, the judge must have the proper
characteristics.

First of all the judge himself must be just. Perfectly
just. If there is a moral blemish in the judge's
character, then chances are his judgments would be
tainted and our quest for perfect justice would fail.

But suppose the judge were totally just but had other
shortcomings. Suppose he had the best intentions and
was morally impeccable but lacked the necessary
knowledge to render a perfect verdict. We can conceive
of a judge who himself is beyond reproach. He is
neither given to bribes or to prejudice. But he doesn't
grasp all the nuances of complex sets of mitigating
circumstances. He could render a verdict to the best of
his ability, but it still may not be perfectly just. Perfect
justice requires a perfect knowledge of every
conceivable mitigating circumstance. It is possible that
perfect justice could happen apart from perfect
knowledge, but it would be by a fortunate accident.
For perfect justice to be insured, the perfect judge

would have to have perfect knowledge. In a word, the perfect judge would have to be *omniscient,* lest some relevant detail escape his notice and distort his verdict.

But suppose our perfect judge acts with perfect integrity and with perfect knowledge and renders a perfect verdict. Is that enough to insure a perfect justice?

Not yet. If a perfect decision is rendered it still must be carried out. Perfect laws do not guarantee perfect behavior. Perfect verdicts do not insure perfect consequences. The prisoner may escape from jail and cheat justice.

For perfect justice to be carried out the judge must have the power necessary to see that it happens. He must have enough power to withstand any attempt to disrupt the flow of justice. There cannot be a single maverick molecule outside the scope of his sovereign power and authority, lest that single molecule become the grain of sand that brings the machine of justice to a grinding halt. The perfect judge must have perfect power. He must be all-powerful, or omnipotent. That is the good news contained in the biblical assertion that "The Lord God Omnipotent reigneth."

If the Lord God Omnipotent does not reign, we have no hope of justice. A Lord God Impotent cannot serve the cause of justice. Nothing less than a morally perfect, omniscient, immutable, eternal, and omnipotent God can insure that our moral sense of obligation is meaningful. No God, no justice. No justice, no ultimate right and wrong. We return to Dostoevsky's conclusion: If there is no God, then all things are permissible.

Such a conclusion leaves man and society no real grounds for ethics. Without an ethical base society becomes impossible to maintain. It may last for the short haul while it is tenuously held together by the remains of theistic norms. But ultimately it will fail by the sheer weight of its intolerable conventions.

Therefore, on practical grounds Kant argued for the existence of God and for life after death, two assumptions that are necessary for the very survival of human society.

Kant realized that such practical considerations do not "prove" the existence of God. They only prove that *if* life is to be meaningful there must be a God who ensures justice. They prove only that *if* my sense of right and wrong are meaningful, then God must exist. Kant said, "We must live *as if* there is a God."

The advantage of Kant's argument is not that it proves the existence of God or life after death. The advantage is found in that it cuts off the heads of all the philosophies that want to have their cake and eat it too. It smashes all the middle-ground views that want to find a resting place somewhere between full-fledged theism and radical nihilism.

It is not by accident that many philosophers since Kant have turned to such a nihilistic philosophy of despair. They argue that we cannot believe in God or life after death simply because the options to these beliefs are so grim. Let's face the music, they say. There is no God. There is no justice. There is no such thing as right and wrong. We live alone in a universe that is neither hostile or beneficent toward our moral decisions. No, it is far worse than that. We live in a universe that is ultimately *indifferent* to human actions. It ultimately doesn't give a tinker's damn because man ultimately isn't worth a tinker's damn.

Every bone in our bodies protests against such a

negative view of human life. Every breath we draw is breathed with the hope that our lives do matter. It is intolerable to our minds that all is futile. We take comfort in the practical speculations of philosophers like Socrates and Kant. But we long for more. We need assurance beyond the mere practical wish that justice be done.

What we need is a word from "out there." We need some tangible evidence that our hope is not a mere illusion based on our inner drive for meaning and significance. We need more than an "as if" to bring us courage.

This is why the "news" of the New Testament is so vital. Here we possess a record that goes beyond speculation to historical reality. Let us turn then to the message and the record of the Christ. Let us hear the message of Jesus of Nazareth and the testimony to His conquest of the grave.

CHAPTER SEVEN
JESUS AND THE AFTERLIFE

To rise above the speculation of philosophers and bypass the occult we must turn our attention to Jesus. No one's teaching on the subject of life after death equals or surpasses that of Jesus of Nazareth. The concept of life beyond the grave was at the core of His teaching message.

One of the best-known words of Jesus on the subject of life after death is found in John 14. Here Jesus is present in the Upper Room for the Last Supper. The discussion recorded takes place on the eve of Christ's crucifixion, shortly before His agony in Gethsemane and His subsequent arrest.

To comfort his friends Jesus declares the following:

*Let not your heart be troubled; you believe in God,
believe also in Me. In My Father's house are many
mansions; if it were not so, I would have told you. I go
to prepare a place for you. And if I go and prepare a
place for you, I will come again and receive you to
Myself; that where I am, there you may be also.*
John 14:1-3

Why should the disciples be gripped by troubled
hearts? In the previous chapter Jesus Himself was
troubled. John tells us that Jesus "was troubled in
spirit" (John 13:21). Jesus was troubled by the
announcement He was about to make of His imminent
betrayal at the hands of Judas.

Imagine the setting. A pall of foreboding gloom
hangs over the Upper Room. Three years of public
ministry, three years of close fellowship among His
disciples had brought them to this hour. It was an hour
of profound crisis. There was much to be troubled
about. A sense of finality hovered about them. Jesus
knew that His hour had come. He revealed His
impending death to His friends. He added to their
apprehension by announcing three very troubling
things. He declared that Judas was going to betray
Him, that Peter was going to deny Him, and, worst of
all, that He was going to leave them.

*Little children, I shall be with you a little while longer.
You will seek Me; and as I said to the Jews so now I
say to you, "Where I am going you cannot come."*
John 13:33

Here Peter exclaimed, "Lord, where are You going?"
Jesus replied, "Where I am going you cannot follow

Me now, but you shall follow Me afterward" (John 13:36).

These words of Christ are packed with historical content. Jesus' relationship with Simon Peter began with two simple words, "Follow Me!" (Matthew 4:19). Peter walked away from his nets and followed Jesus. He literally followed Jesus. Whenever Jesus went, Peter went. He was with Jesus at the wedding feast of Cana. He was with Jesus on the Mount of Transfiguration. He even followed Jesus walking on the water. Now the time of following was abruptly over. Jesus said, "You cannot follow Me now."

One of the most difficult dimensions a person experiences as he approaches death is the troubling knowledge that the journey must be made alone, without human companionship. We can sit by the bedside of our loved ones. We can hold their hands and they can hold ours. But a moment comes when separation takes place. It is that separation, however temporary, that distresses our spirits. Often at the precise moment of death, when the last breath is taken and the heartbeat falls silent, the announcement is made, "He's gone!" We describe death as a departure, a separation.

When Elijah was being cared for by the widow of Zarephath, the widow's son became seriously ill and died. The Old Testament records that Elijah raised the son from the dead. But before the miracle took place the woman berated Elijah in her distress. She cried out to him, "What have I to do with you, O man of God? Have you come to me to bring my sin to remembrance, and to kill my son?" (1 Kings 17:18).

Elijah responded with a command: "Give me your son." Then the Scripture says that Elijah took him out of her arms and carried him to the upper room where he was staying (1 Kings 17:19).

Before Elijah performed the miracle he had to take the dead boy out of his mother's arms. It is obvious from the text that in her grief the woman was desperately hanging on to the corpse of her child. Elijah had to pry them apart.

The scene is not uncommon. We want to hold on to our loved ones as long as possible. The moment of separation is almost unbearable.

Even this postscript is enigmatic. What did Jesus mean about following Him afterward? Peter probably understood these words to mean, "You cannot follow Me in death, now. But afterwards you shall also die."

The question then is this: Where was Peter to follow? Was it merely to follow Jesus to the grave? Jesus answers that question in John 14. When He said, "Let not your heart be troubled," He gave a reason for His command.

First He called them to an act of faith. He said, "You believe in God, believe also in Me" (John 14:1). He was saying simply, "Trust Me." Jesus does not ask for a leap of blind faith. When He asked His disciples to trust Him, there was a backlog of history to support His request. It was as if Jesus were saying, "Look, I've never let you down. My Father has never broken a promise. I haven't either. I have proven Myself to be trustworthy. Now, when I go away, it's time to trust Me on the force of My promise. You believe in God, now believe in Me. The key to putting your troubled hearts to rest is to trust Me for the future."

This is the heart of Christianity. This is why we speak of the Christian *faith*, not the Christian *religion*. Religion has to do with the outward cultic practices of human beings. Christianity, the Christian faith, has to do with trusting God for your very life. The step Jesus is asking His disciples to take is a big step. It is one thing to believe *in* God; it is quite another to *believe* God. This is a major step in practice, though in theory it should not require any step at all. Our distinction between believing *in* God and believing God should be a distinction without a difference, a sheer exercise in sophistry. In truth, if we really believe in God, we will believe whatever God tells us.

Yet in terms of concrete reality there is often a gap between our theoretical faith in God and our actual trust in what He says. Our faith is not pure. Like gold that is marred by dross, so our faith is often mixed with doubt. We cry out, "Lord, I believe, help my unbelief!"

At the moment of death, fear and doubt can assault the heart and press hard against our faith. It is at that moment that we must hear the words of Jesus, "Trust Me."

Preparing a Place in the Father's House

Jesus now declares the substance of the "where" that the disciples will ultimately follow: "In My Father's house are many mansions. . . . I go to prepare a place for you" (John 14:2).

At age twelve Jesus had confounded the theologians in the temple. When His anxious parents found Him there, they scolded Him, "Son, why have You done this to us? Look, Your father and I have sought You anxiously" (Luke 2:48).

The boy Jesus replied with a thinly veiled rebuke of His anxiety-stricken mother: "Why is it that you sought Me? Did you not know that I must be about My Father's business?" (Luke 2:49).

The Father's business took place in the temple. Later Jesus referred to the temple in Jerusalem as His Father's house. "Do not make My Father's house a house of merchandise!" (John 2:16).

In John 14 Jesus speaks again of His Father's house. He is no longer referring to the temple in Jerusalem. The temple was the earthly house of God. That house was perishable and indeed was destroyed. Here Jesus speaks of the heavenly Jerusalem, the ultimate house of His Father.

Jesus promises His disciples that they will one day follow Him to the Father's house in heaven. He declares that, "I go to prepare a place for you." Jesus explains that His departure from their midst, which was troubling their hearts, should be an occasion of great joy. Jesus left them to go to prepare their rooms in heaven.

Jesus not only makes it possible for us to go to heaven, he has actually gone there to assure our reservations and prepare our rooms for us.

I spend about nine months of the year away from my home. Doing so much traveling has a long-range impact on me. I've noticed several patterns emerging in my own psyche about traveling. For one thing, I'm more fussy about advance reservations.

On our trip to heaven we have the best of all possible advance accommodations, prepared by the best of all possible advance men. Jesus Himself has gone before us to prepare a place in our Father's house.

There are few things more frustrating for a weary

traveler than to arrive at a hotel and discover that the hotel has failed to record your reservation or has given your room to somebody else. These mix-ups do occur and are maddening when they happen. But it cannot possibly happen in heaven. If we belong to Christ then we have a rock solid reservation. There are many rooms in the Father's house. There is a place for us that no one else can take away.

An "Adult" View of Eternal Life

I think that the most comforting words Jesus ever spoke about heaven are found in John 14:2. Jesus said, "If it were not so, I would have told you."

The tone of this utterance has a paternal ring to it. Jesus is speaking as a Father speaks to his children. We note that moments earlier Jesus had addressed his disciples as "little children." "Little children, I shall be with you a little while longer" (John 13:33). There comes a time in children's lives that parents must tell them the facts of life. Infants must be weaned away from the realm of fairy tales and myths. The day of sober truth arrives when a child becomes too old to maintain a belief in Santa Claus and the Easter Bunny. A transaction takes place that involves the demythologizing of life. What is fun and enchanting for children must give way to preparation for the harsh realities of adulthood. There is a time when childish things must be put away. The apostle declared,

When I was a child, I spoke as a child, I understood as a child, I thought as a child; but when I became a man, I put away childish things. 1 Corinthians 13:11

If a man fails to put away childish things, he faces adulthood severely handicapped. To hang on to childhood myths too long is to be crippled intellectually.

Jesus understood that if His disciples were going to be able to carry out their mission as adults, if they were going to be able to face the tribulations that were certainly going to be theirs, they had to be able to discern the difference between myth and reality.

As a teacher, Jesus, like any other teacher, had to have His pupils unlearn mistaken ideas they carried into His classroom. Education involves far more than acquiring new information. True education involves the often painful process of discarding pet ideas and theories that will not hold up under critical scrutiny. Jesus' teaching involved correction of erroneous concepts.

Here He announces that one of their pet concepts was in no need of correction. The disciples' hope for life after death was not a myth or a fantasy. Their conviction of eternal life was not based on an illusory form of wish-projection. There was nothing childish about it.

It is normal for a child who has experienced the trauma of the loss of Santa Claus to wonder about the rest of the things his parents have taught him. What about God? What about heaven? Are these part of the fairy tale world I must give up?

In light of this crisis of doubt Jesus declared, "If it were not so, I would have told you." This declaration is a negative form of divine revelation. Baleful existential theologians to the contrary, it may be received as propositional truth. The statement comes in the literary form of a conditional "If—then" statement. What is in view here is a simple condition contrary to fact.

Jesus was saying this: If your faith in a future life was not valid, I would have corrected your false hopes. But the fact of the matter is that there is a heaven and you can count on it. I would not have left so weighty a false idea go uncorrected.

Here is a dogmatic utterance par excellence. Jesus speaks to this point not merely as a highly skilled and knowledgeable rabbi, nor even as an anointed prophet of God. He speaks with the absolute and infallible authority of the Son of God. We recall that Jesus declared boldly that "All authority has been given to Me in heaven and on earth" (Matthew 28:18).

The Matter of Jesus' Authority

If this boldest of all human claims is correct, then Jesus' statements on heaven provide the highest and most trustworthy source of information we could ever find on the subject of heaven. We notice that He said that He had been given all authority in heaven. Now, if the One who possesses all authority in heaven speaks a word about heaven, then it follows that His teaching on the subject is impeccable. Here we have it in unimpeachable authority.

Jesus claimed to receive His authority from the source of all authority, indeed the author of authority, God Himself. John the Baptist bore witness to Jesus' authority by saying

He who comes from above is above all; he who is of the earth is earthly and speaks of the earth. He who comes from heaven is above all. . . . For He whom

*God has sent speaks the words of God, for God does
not give the Spirit by measure.* John 3:31-34

Jesus added to this claim:

*My doctrine is not Mine, but His who sent Me. . . .
You both know Me, and you know where I am from;
and I have not come of Myself, but He who sent Me is
true, whom you do not know. But I know Him, for I
am from Him, and He sent Me.* John 7:16, 28-29

*I have many things to say and to judge concerning
you, but He who sent Me is true; and I speak to the
world those things which I heard from Him . . . I do
nothing of Myself; but as My Father taught Me, I
speak these things.* John 8:26-28

When we receive important information, whether
from the news media or from a scholarly textbook, we
are urged to "consider the source." We seek
documentation of our data to insure that the
information is credible. The source Jesus claims for
His information is the same source He claims for His
authority, namely God Himself.

Jesus' contemporaries, including those who were
hostile toward Him, were often confounded by His
manner of speaking.

*And so it was, when Jesus had ended these sayings,
that the people were astonished at His teaching, for He
taught them as one having authority, and not as the
Scribes.* Matthew 7:28-29

*Now some of them wanted to take Him, but no one
laid hands on Him. Then the officers came to the chief
priests and Pharisees, who said to them, "Why have
you not brought Him?" The officers answered, "No
man ever spoke like this Man!"* John 7:44-46

Jesus spoke as one having authority. The Greek
word that is used here for "authority" is the word
exousia. The term *exousia* is made up of a prefix *ex*,
meaning "from" or "out of" and the root *ousia*, which
is the present participle of the verb "to be." Literally
the word means "out of being" or "substance."

Our dictionaries render the term *exousia* to mean
"authority" or "power." There is an element of both
ideas compressed within the word *exousia*. We can
translate it as "powerful authority." It is an authority
based on substance, or being.

In simple terms, what the Bible means when it says
that Jesus spoke as One having authority is that Jesus
was not uttering an empty or vaporous opinion. He
had the "stuff" or the "substance" of reality behind His
words. His authority was backed up by nothing less
than the very being or substance of God.

When God speaks, all dispute about the truth and
reality of what is spoken must end, except for those
who are chronically obstreperous, or incomprehensibly
foolish. Who else would dare to correct the Deity?

If Jesus spoke the truth concerning His authority,
then no objection can withstand the conclusion that
He spoke the truth regarding life after death. His
declaration, "If it were not so, I would have told you,"
remains the consolation of all consolations.

The Ultimate Comfort for the Bereaved

The bringing of comfort to the bereaved is a task each of us faces from time to time. It is often an unenviable and intimidating task. A funeral parlor is a stage where the most accomplished speaker stutters. We feel so inadequate to the task of finding the right words to say to those in mourning.

Recently I visited the funeral parlor where my first employer's wife was laid out for final viewing. My employer hired me as a shoe shine boy when I was fourteen. I worked alongside him in his cobbler's shop. Over the years I have kept in touch with him and count him a friend. When I visited the funeral home I had no words of wisdom to offer. All I could think to do was to sit by his side quietly for an hour or so. All I had to offer him was my presence, an unspoken testimony to my care for him in his hour of grief.

I remained silent on that occasion because I had no words to say that I thought were adequate to the need. My vocabulary failed me. I do not speak exousia about anything.

When Jesus went to the home of Mary and Martha on the occasion of their brother Lazarus's death, He consoled them with words of exousia. He declared to Martha, "Your brother will rise again" (John 11:23).

Martha understood Jesus' words to refer to the future hope of resurrection: "I know that he will rise again in the resurrection at the last day" (John 11:24).

To this Jesus replied: "I am the resurrection and the life. He who believes on Me, though he may die, he shall live. And whoever lives and believes in Me shall never die. Do you believe this?" (John 11:25-26).

Jesus of Nazareth never uttered a bolder statement

than this. He directly linked eternal life with Himself. He tied everlasting life, ultimate victory over the greatest enemy of all mankind, death itself, with faith in Him. To believe in Christ is to gain eternal life.

There are few people in the history of the world who ever dared to make such a claim. Only one backed up the claim with action.

Far beyond the words of Jesus stands the record of His deeds. His example matches the power of His words. Only moments after His words of comfort to Martha, Jesus went to the grave of Lazarus. Martha protested against the removal of the stone that sealed the entrance. Lazarus had been dead for four days. Presumably he had not been embalmed. Martha shrunk in horror at the expected stench of the corpse of her brother.

When the stone was removed, Jesus uttered a command in a loud voice. By divine imperative He ordered Lazarus back from death: "Lazarus, come forth!"

Lazarus was bound hand and foot with grave clothes. His soul had departed and was bound as tightly by the grip of death. At the command of Jesus, death released its grip. Lazarus's heart began to beat. Blood started to flow afresh in his veins. Decomposing tissue was instantly restored to vibrant health. Lazarus became conscious. He was suddenly mobile. Despite the constricting grave clothes he walked out of his tomb. Jesus gave another command: "Loose him and let him go" (John 11:44).

What Jesus did for Lazarus, for Jairus's daughter, and for the widow of Nain's son was also accomplished in His own body. On the day of his death Jesus was taunted by mockers who cried, "He saved others; let Him save Himself if He is the Christ, the chosen of God" (Luke 23:35).

Jesus knew that in His hour of death He had a legion of angels who could rescue Him in a moment. A simple word from Christ would have been enough to mobilize the angelic forces in His behalf. But His duty was to die. He drank the cup and with His final words entrusted Himself to His Father.

For three days the Son of God was dead. For three days the Father was silent. For three days those who mocked Jesus felt triumph in their hostility toward Him. For three days, His friends and disciples mourned their incomparable loss. For three days they hid in fear and bewilderment.

Then the Lord God omnipotent broke the silence. He did not scream. There was no trumpet heralding. There was quietness in the garden, broken only by the soft weeping of Mary Magdalene. Mary was distressed by the discovery that Jesus' body was missing from the tomb. His corpse had disappeared in what seemed to her to be the final and most senseless assault against His dignity. Someone, she assumed, had stolen the body of Christ.

Someone was standing behind her. She thought it was the gardener. He spoke: "Woman, why are you weeping? Whom are you seeking?" (John 20:15). Mary replied, "Sir, if you have carried Him away, tell me where you have laid Him, and I will take Him away" (John 20:15b).

Then Mary heard the man speak her name. "Mary!" He said. Instant recognition flooded her soul at the sound of His voice. She turned and exclaimed simply, "Rabboni!" which means "teacher."

This was the birth of faith that was the nativity of the Christian faith. "He is risen" was the first creed of Christendom.

The resurrection of Christ is the central affirmation of the Christian church. With its truth stands or falls the whole of Christian religion. If there is no resurrection there is no Christianity. If there is no resurrection there is no reason to continue the church, save as one more social agency cloaking humanitarian services in mythical religious garb.

This is not to say that there have not been numerous attempts to construct a resurrectionless Christianity. In the nineteenth century so-called liberal Christians tried to modernize the Christian faith by stripping it of its "nonessential" miraculous husk and reducing it to its ethical kernel. The supernatural elements were rejected in an attempt to offer a religion of values that would enhance life in this world without getting caught up in an otherworldly fixation on pie-in-the-sky. Jesus became for them the supreme model of brotherly love who demonstrated an altruistic self-sacrifice that ended with his heroic death. Jesus the Savior from death and the Victor over the grave, became Jesus the human teacher of ethics.

Such a Jesus has no need of a church. Worship is at best a hollow service, and at worst an act of blasphemy, if it is directed toward a dead teacher of morality. We have no church for Socrates. We sing no hymns to Cicero. We say no prayers to Aristotle.

Paul's Nine-point Argument for Resurrection

Attempts to create a Christianity without a resurrection began early in the church's history. The

Apostle Paul had to confront the problem in the troublesome Corinthian church. His apostolic response to it is as noteworthy as it is timeless. The apostle's rebuke to the Corinthian congregation is as relevant today as it was when it was first given. Perhaps even more relevant, as what once was a local problem restricted to an isolated situation is now an epidemic in the church of the twentieth century.

The apostle addressed the Corinthians with a crucial question: "Now if Christ is preached that He has been raised from the dead, how do some among you say that there is no resurrection of the dead?" (1 Corinthians 15:12).

Here we find members of the early Christian community who denied life after death. Their rejection was categorical and absolute. They insisted that there is no resurrection from the dead. No one, not even Jesus, survives the grave.

Paul responded to this view by stepping into his opponents' shoes to demonstrate the radical inconsistency and utter absurdity of a Christian faith without resurrection.

Let us follow closely the apostle's argument. He spells out the logical implications of no resurrection. He moves in a progressive manner, mounting point after point of negative implications that follow an irresistible logic.

POINT 1

But if there is no resurrection of the dead, then Christ is not risen. 1 Corinthians 15:13

Who can argue with such logic? If we have a universal negative proposition (no resurrection of the

dead) there allows for no exception. The laws of
immediate inference do not allow a "none" coupled
with a "some." Here we find a conditional proposition
where the conclusion cannot be refuted. If A is true,
then B must also be true. If there is no resurrection of
the dead, then, manifestly, Christ is not risen.

POINT 2

*If Christ is not risen, then our preaching is vain and
your faith is also vain.* 1 Corinthians 15:14

Here Paul sets himself against all forms of
liberalized Christianity that seek to deny the
resurrection of Christ on the one hand and continue to
preach and call people to "faith" on the other hand. In
Paul's view this is a foolish attempt to have your cake
and eat it too. He views this as an absurd exercise in
futility. Without a real resurrection Christian
preaching is useless.

Paul does not commit the fallacy of a false dilemma
here. He sees the issue as a genuine case of the
either/or. Either Christ is raised or preaching and faith
are useless.

POINT 3

*Yes, and we are found false witnesses of God, because
we have testified of God that He raised up Christ,
whom He did not raise up—if in fact the dead do not
rise.* 1 Corinthians 15:15

If ever the apostle ran the risk of insulting his
readers by laboring the obvious, it is here. For Paul to
add the last portion of this sentence ("whom He did

not raise up—if in fact the dead do not rise") is to spell out the most obvious of conclusions. I sense a hint of sarcasm here dripping from the apostle's pen. Nothing could be simpler to understand then the conclusion that if the dead do not rise then God did not raise Christ. But there is a more ominous note here. Paul is writing as a Jewish theologian. He is acutely aware of the seriousness of bearing false witness. To bear false witness against men was a capital offense proscribed in the Ten Commandments. To bear false witness against God is an even more serious offense.

Paul's reasoning is this: If Christ is not raised, then Paul and the other apostles must be judged as false prophets. They would be members of Jehovah's False Witnesses. To deny the apostolic proclamation of the resurrection while at the same time extolling their virtues as teachers of ethics is to praise the folly of false prophets. The apostle himself sees this as a hopeless contradiction. He sees himself disqualified as a trusted teacher if his witness to the resurrection is false. Here Paul puts his and the other apostles' total reputation and integrity on the line. It is as if Paul said, "Take me or leave me on this point."

POINT 4

And if Christ is not risen, your faith is futile; you are still in your sins! 1 Corinthians 15:17

Again the apostle presses the point of futility. Without resurrection the Christian faith is futile. It is useless, a waste of time, energy, and devotion. To believe in a false hope is to set the heart on a course for ultimate frustration. Without the resurrection we are left with no hope. All we have to show for our pilgrimage is unresolved guilt.

Paul sees the resurrection as God's clear sign of His acceptance of Christ's sacrifice as an atonement for our sins. If He is not raised we remain in our sins. We have no Savior. Both our faith and Christ's death are equally useless. We remain debtors who cannot pay our debts.

POINT 5

Then also those who have fallen asleep in Christ have perished. 1 Corinthians 15:18

Of the negative implications of no resurrection, this is perhaps the most grim of all. Paul does not shrink from the brutal conclusion that accompanies the end of all hope. Dante described the sign that was posted on the doorway of hell: *Abandon hope all ye who enter here.* Paul places that sign right here, right now. It is posted not at the gate of hell but at the door of every funeral home.

Every person who has lost a loved one to death knows the poignant hope that abides: it is the hope that somewhere, sometime we will see our loved ones again. That hope is the consolation we cling to when death separates us from our loved ones.

Recently I sat with my daughter and her husband in the delivery room of a hospital maternity ward. My daughter had just given birth to a little girl. The baby was stillborn. In cases like this it is the policy of the hospital to allow the mother and father to hold the dead infant for awhile. Pictures are taken. The baby's footprints are recorded in ink. The baby is named and a record is made of the weight and length of the child. A lock of hair is attached to the record sheet. The certificate with its data is given to the parents when the child is removed to be prepared for burial. The paper is called a "certificate of remembrance."

My daughter came home from the hospital with photos and a certificate of remembrance. She also came home with the profound hope that sometime she will see her daughter again, alive.

Yet, Paul reasons, if Christ is not raised, then those who have died have perished forever. It is the fate of all men to recite the mournful refrain of Edgar Allan Poe's *The Raven:* "Nevermore."

POINT 6

Paul continues by showing the radical inconsistency of those who practiced baptism for the dead in Corinth.

Otherwise, what will they do who are baptized for the dead, if the dead do not rise at all? Why then are they baptized for the dead? 1 Corinthians 15:29

This passing reference to baptism for the dead is the only New Testament reference to such a practice. It has evoked all kinds of consternation. Here Paul neither commends nor condemns the practice. He merely acknowledges that it is practiced among the Corinthians and shows the absurdity of it, if in fact there is no resurrection. To baptize the dead if there is no resurrection would be a waste of time and a waste of water.

POINT 7

*And why do we stand in jeopardy every hour? I
affirm, by the boasting in you which I have in Christ
Jesus our Lord, I die daily. If, in the manner of men, I
have fought with beasts at Ephesus, what advantage is
it to me?* 1 Corinthians 15:30-32a

Here we find a fascinating application. The apostle
turns to his own ministry as evidence of his conviction
that the resurrection "makes sense" out of his own
trials. He uses exceptionally strong language for a Jew.
He affirms his position by taking an oath on his
ministry in Christ. Such oath-taking is not a casual
matter for a pious Jew. He testifies that his own
ministry would be worthless apart from the
resurrection. For a summary of the herculean pain and
effort that marked Paul's ministry, the reader might
take a few moments to read 2 Corinthians 11. Here he
gives a brief record of his suffering in the ministry.

A popular argument for the resurrection goes
something like this: Which is more difficult to believe,
that Christ rose from the dead or that the apostles
were willing to die for a hoax?

I've never found such arguments very satisfying. On
the surface we must admit that though it is rare to find
fanatics who are so deluded that they are willing to die
for something that is not true, or even for something
they know is not true, it is not as rare as a resurrection
from the dead.

An appeal to Paul's extraordinary devotion to his
ministry and his willingness to die for his faith does
not prove conclusively that his faith was valid. What it

does show, however, is that his behavior was indeed consistent with what we might expect from someone who was an eyewitness of the resurrected Jesus. What was true of Paul was true of the other apostles as well. They lived and died in the full confidence of the resurrection of Christ.

POINT 8

If the dead do not rise, "Let us eat and drink, for tomorrow we die." 1 Corinthians 15:32b

Here Paul cuts through all the trappings of religious sentimentality and altruism. He echoes the creed of the ancient Epicurean. If there is no life after death the only present, sensible life-style is that of the blatant hedonist. We might as well grab all the pleasure we can before we are swallowed by final pain. Here is the apostolic anticipation of modern skepticism: Grab all the gusto you can because you only go around once; or, Whoever dies with the most toys, wins.

POINT 9

Though it comes earlier in Paul's argument, I've saved it for last.

If in this life only we have hope in Christ, we are of all men the most pitiable. 1 Corinthians 15:19

Paul could hardly protest louder against all attempts to construct a Christian religion without resurrection. If the value of Christian hope is restricted to this life, then Christians are the most miserable of all people.

Their misery is this: They live a life based on false hope. That hope is a controlling hope. It involves an ethic of postponed reward, an ethic of present sacrifice for the sake of future reward.

Paul is saying that if you are hostile toward Christians perhaps it would be more compassionate to exchange your hostility for pity. Christians who live with deluded hope need pity. They need pity because they are indeed the most pitiable of all people.

The Basis of Eyewitnesses

The most important dimension of Paul's argument for the resurrection is this: It does not rest simply on a speculative basis of grim options. Paul is not concluding that since life without resurrection is miserable we should therefore take a deep breath, close our eyes, and conjure up faith in a resurrection. Paul does not say, we must live *as if* there were a resurrection because without it all these bad conclusions must be faced. His nine-point argument is merely corroborative. It is a study in consistency and inconsistency. It is not the basis of his confidence in the resurrection of Christ.

Paul's case for the resurrection goes far beyond speculative philosophy. He provides evidence that neither Plato nor Kant could offer. He appeals to eyewitness testimony to the historical reality of Jesus' resurrection:

For I delivered to you first of all that which I also received; that Christ died for our sins according to the Scriptures, and that He was buried, and that He rose again the third day according to the Scriptures, and

that He was seen by Cephas, then by the twelve. After that He was seen by over five hundred brethren at once, of whom the greater part remain to the present, but some have fallen asleep. After that He was seen by James, then by all the apostles. Then last of all He was seen by me also, as by one born out of due time.
1 Corinthians 15:3-8

This is the record of history concerning Jesus of Nazareth. His life, His death, His burial, and His resurrection were all foretold by Scripture. Testimony to His resurrection was not based on inferences or conclusions drawn from the appearance of an empty tomb. A missing corpse was not enough. It was based on the appearance of Jesus—alive, not to one or two people, but to a host of people.

Paul names the people who saw Jesus return from the grave alive. These are people who include those who saw Him die. It includes those who witnessed the crucifixion and final spear thrust in the side. It includes people who saw the corpse be prepared for burial.

The group of eyewitnesses included one that numbered over five hundred people on a single occasion. When Paul noted that to the Corinthians, he claimed that most of the eyewitnesses were still alive. It was as if he said, "Check it out. The witnesses can still be cross-examined."

We do not have the opportunity now to cross-examine the five hundred. But we still have the written record of the apostolic eyewitnesses. We can still read John's account or Matthew's.

Finally Paul declares that he personally saw the resurrected Christ. Paul's words are thrilling. Not to be satisfied with secondhand reports, the apostle declares: "He was seen by me also."

"I saw Him!" That's what Plato and Kant could never say.

It is no wonder that Paul exuded confidence in the victory of Christ over death. His final conclusion follows irresistibly from his stirring testimony:

Therefore, my beloved brethren, be steadfast, immovable, always abounding in the work of the Lord, knowing that your labor is not in vain in the Lord. 1 Corinthians 15:58

Paul's "therefore" signals the grand conclusion. There is reason—solid ground for the solemn admonition. *Be steadfast.* With the certainty of resurrection, steadfastness is called for. Vacillation is not the mark of those who know the resurrected Christ. The resurrection provides the anchor for the soul that makes it an immovable object. *Always abounding in the work of the Lord.* The resurrection sparks work in abundance. It is labor that rests in the certainty that no effort made in Christ is futile effort. Our labor, our pain, our suffering—yea, even our dying—are not in vain.

CHAPTER EIGHT
TO DIE IS GAIN

Blaise Pascal once observed that a crucial element of man's misery is found in this: He can always contemplate a better life than it is possible for him to achieve. We all have the ability to dream, to allow our imaginations to soar in free flight of fancy. Yet when we push our imaginative powers to their limit, we crash into the barrier of the unknown. Who can imagine what heaven is really like? It is beyond our ken. It is beyond our most ambitious dreams.

One sage remarked that if we could imagine the most pleasant experience possible and thought about doing it for eternity, we would be conceiving of something that would be closer to hell than to heaven.

We simply cannot fathom a situation of absolute felicity. We have no concrete reference point for it.

It is the mysterious, uncharted realm of the afterlife that provoked Hamlet to declare

Who would fardels bear,
To grunt and sweat under a weary life,
But that the dread of something after death,
The undiscovered country, from whose bourn
No traveler returns, puzzles the will,
And makes us rather bear those ills we have
Than fly to others that we know not of?
Thus conscience does make cowards of us all.
Hamlet, Act III, Scene I

It is the unknown quality of the afterlife that makes us rather bear those ills we have than fly to others we know not of. Perhaps Hamlet had a sense of the flip-side of Pascal's observation. Not only do we have the ability to contemplate a better existence than we presently enjoy; we also have the power to imagine a worse existence than we presently endure.

Our imaginings about the afterlife are restricted primarily to analogy. To move beyond this world is to move into another dimension. That different dimension involves both continuity and discontinuity. Insofar as there is continuity we can think by way of analogies drawn from this world. The elements of discontinuity remain inscrutable. We simply cannot grasp what goes beyond our points of reference.

Though the Bible is somewhat oblique about our future state, it is not altogether silent. We are given hints, vital clues about what heaven is like. There is a kind of tantalizing foretaste of future glory that is set before us. There is a partial unveiling that gives us a glimpse behind the dark glass.

There are a few points about heaven that are revealed to us with utmost clarity. Before we turn our attention to the vivid images depicted in the Apocalypse of John, let us examine some of the didactic assertions made about heaven in the Gospels and the Epistles.

Better Than Life on Earth

The first lesson we learn about heaven is that life in heaven is better than life on earth. The Apostle Paul declares:

For I know that this will turn out for my salvation through your prayer and the supply of the Spirit of Jesus Christ, according to my earnest expectation and hope that in nothing I shall be ashamed, but that with all boldness, as always, so now also Christ will be magnified in my body, whether by life or by death. For to me, to live is Christ, and to die is gain. But if I live on in the flesh, this will mean fruit from my labor; yet what I shall choose I cannot tell. For I am hard pressed between the two, having a desire to depart and be with Christ, which is far better. Nevertheless to remain in the flesh is more needful for you.
Philippians 1:19-24

Paul speaks of death as *gain*. We tend to think of death as *loss*. To be sure, the death of a loved one involves a loss for those who are left behind. But for the one who passes from this world to heaven it is a gain.

Paul does not despise life in this world. He says that he is "hard pressed" between choosing to remain and desiring to depart. The contrast he points to between this life and heaven is not a contrast between the bad and the good. The comparison is between the *good* and the *better*. This life in Christ is good. Life in heaven is better. Yet he takes it a step farther. He declares that to depart and be with Christ is *far better* (v. 23). The transition to heaven involves more than a slight or marginal improvement. The gain is great. Heaven is far better than life in this world.

This echoes the comparison Paul makes to the Corinthians:

For our light affliction, which is but for a moment, is working for us a far more exceeding and eternal weight of glory, while we do not look at the things which are seen, but at the things which are not seen. For the things which are seen are temporary, but the things which are not seen are eternal. For we know that if our earthly house, this tent, is destroyed, we have a building from God, a house not made with hands, eternal in the heavens. For in this we groan, earnestly desiring to be clothed with our habitation which is from heaven, if indeed having been clothed, we shall not be found naked. For we who are in this tent groan, being burdened, not because we want to be unclothed, but further clothed, that mortality may be swallowed up by life. Now He who has prepared us for this very thing is God, who also has given us the Spirit as a guarantee. 2 Corinthians 4:17–5:5

The contrast Paul develops here is between the temporary and the permanent, between the temporal and the eternal.

The Resurrection of the Body

Paul looks to the ultimate hope of future bliss that includes the resurrection of our bodies. The Apostles' Creed contains the affirmation "I believe in the resurrection of the body." This article of faith does not focus on the resurrection of Christ's body, but upon the resurrection of our own bodies. Christ's resurrection is the precursor of our own. He is the first fruits of all who will participate in resurrection (1 Corinthians 15:20-23).

Paul elaborates the theme of our resurrected bodies as his ringing conclusion to 1 Corinthians 15.

But someone will say, "How are the dead raised up? And with what body do they come?" Foolish one, what you sow is not made alive unless it dies. And what you sow, you do not sow that body that shall be, but mere grain—perhaps wheat or some other grain. But God gives it a body as He pleases, and to each seed its own body. 1 Corinthians 15:35-38

Paul presents an analogy drawn from agriculture. The transition we will experience between this life and the resurrection life is likened into that of a seed that germinates. For a seed to burst forth into life it must first be buried. It must decay. The seed rots before the grass can flower. What emerges from the ground far exceeds in glory what was planted as a seed.

The apostle continues the analogy by referring to the wide diversity of bodies and forms by which life in this world is manifested.

All flesh is not the same flesh, but there is one kind of flesh of men, another flesh of beasts, another of fish, and another of birds. There are also celestial bodies

*and terrestrial bodies, but the glory of the celestial is
one, and the glory of the terrestrial is another. There is
one glory of the sun, another glory of the moon, and
another glory of the stars; for one star differs from
another star in glory.* 1 Corinthians 15:39-41

Paul cites a rising crescendo of levels of glory that
are found in the created realm. He hints of that glory
that for the present remains unseen. His reasoning
suggests something like this: In our limited view of the
totality of reality we glimpse but a small portion of
what is actually there. Our scope is at best myopic. We
are spiritually nearsighted. Imagine the arrogance to
assume that life in its fullest dimension is exhausted by
the scope of our limited vision. If we consider for a
moment the knowledge that we do have of the vast
universe in which we live, we realize that the borders
of our experience are infinitesimal. Our experience of
the natural order is smaller than a droplet in a vast
ocean. And even if we grasped the full measure of the
natural order, that would not give us penetration into
the supernatural realm. But the lesson is this: The
pinpoint of reality we do perceive is enough to scream
that there is much, much more to the diversity of life
we already experience.

Now Paul moves to the way of contrast:

*So also is the resurrection of the dead. The body is
sown in corruption, it is raised in incorruption. It is
sown in dishonor, it is raised in glory. It is sown in
weakness, it is raised in power. It is sown a natural
body, it is raised a spiritual body. There is a natural
body, and there is a spiritual body.* 1 Corinthians
15:42-44

The contrast between the earthly body and the resurrected body is vivid. It includes these elements:

Natural Body	Resurrected Body
Corruption	Incorruption
Dishonor	Glory
Weakness	Power
Natural	Spiritual

Corruption, dishonor, and weakness are all qualities with which we are familiar. They are a normal part of our everyday experience. They are all attributes of our natural bodies. These qualities will give way in the resurrection to their antithesis. Incorruption, glory, and power are the characteristics of the spiritual body.

What a Spiritual Body Is Like

The term *spiritual body* sounds discordant to the ear. We tend to think of spirit and body as mutually exclusive polar opposites. But Paul is not resorting to contradictions to make his point. He is referring to a spiritualized body that has been transformed from its natural limitations. It is a glorified body, a body that is raised in a new dimension.

The only real clue we have to this type of spiritual body is the sketchy view we have of the resurrected body of Jesus. We know that the body Jesus had after His resurrection was different from the body that was buried. It manifested both continuity and discontinuity. We read of people having some difficulty recognizing Him, yet, at the same time, recognition did occur. Jesus ate breakfast with His disciples. He showed the marks of His crucifixion to Thomas. He said to him:

Reach your finger here, and look at my hands; and reach your hand here, and put it into My side. Do not be unbelieving, but believing. John 20:27

Whether or not Thomas did as he was instructed is not recorded in the gospel, but presumably the opportunity was there for him to do it. John also records a cryptic statement about Jesus that has fueled much speculation about His resurrected body.

And after eight days His disciples were again inside, and Thomas with them. Jesus came, the doors being shut, and stood in the midst, and said, "Peace to you!" John 20:26

Why does John record the phrase "the doors being shut"? Is the phrase included to tell us something about the disciples, or to tell us something about the resurrected body of Jesus? On the surface it seems like an insignificant detail. Perhaps all John had in mind was to emphasize the state of fearfulness that characterized the disciples after the crucifixion. It seems as though they spent a lot of time indoors. In verse 19 he mentioned, "When the doors were shut where the disciples were assembled, for fear of the Jews, Jesus came and stood in their midst."

We can possibly reconstruct the scene in this way: The disciples, in a state of fright, were huddled together with the door shut. While they were preoccupied with their fear and consternation, Jesus came to their place of assembly, quietly opened the door, and came in and spoke to them. In this scenario the reference to the shut door tells us nothing about the resurrected body of Jesus other than it could walk around and open doors.

On the other hand, perhaps John is hinting that Jesus appeared in the middle of the room *without* opening the door. This would mean that His resurrected body had the capacity to move unimpeded through solid objects. The text does not explicitly say that. Such an inference is possible from the text, but it is by no means demanded from the text. It remains a matter of conjecture.

What is certain is that Paul looks to Jesus as the exemplar of what our resurrected bodies will be like:

As so it is written, "The first man Adam became a living being." The last Adam became a life-giving spirit. However, the spiritual is not first, but the natural, and afterward the spiritual. The first man was of the earth, made of dust; the second Man is the Lord from heaven. As was the man of dust, so also are those who are made of dust; and as is the heavenly Man, so also are those who are heavenly. And as we have borne the image of the man of dust, we shall also bear the image of the heavenly Man. 1 Corinthians 15:45-49

All we who are human partake of the earthly nature of Adam. We are children of the dust. Our bodies suffer from all the weaknesses and frailties that belong to the earth. Our new natures will involve a tabernacle made in heaven. In the heavenly body there is no room for cancer or heart disease. The curse of the fall will be removed. We will be clothed after the image and likeness of the New Adam, the heavenly Man. We will still be men. There will be continuity. Our personal identities will remain intact. We will be recognizable as the persons we are. But there will also be discontinuity as the shackles of the dust will be liberated by the heavenly form.

Continuity and Discontinuity

One vexing problem we face as we speculate about
heaven is the question of recognition. We recognize
people by their physical characteristics. Some of the
most obvious characteristics include matters of age
and weight. Will a person who dies in infancy look like
a baby forever? Will the aged remain wrinkled in
countenance? Will I be fat or thin, tall or short?

To ask such questions (which we can hardly resist
asking) is to run head-on into the barriers of our
understanding of the elements of discontinuity. I
assume (and that is all it is, an assumption) that
somehow these questions will flee from relevance once
we transcend the realm of the dust and enter into our
glorified states.

Paul insists that though we will surely maintain
continuity with our present personal identities, we will
nevertheless undergo the changes of transformation.

*Now this I say, brethren, that flesh and blood cannot
inherit the kingdom of God; nor does corruption
inherit incorruption. Behold, I tell you a mystery: We
shall not all sleep, but we shall all be changed—in a
moment, in the twinkling of an eye, at the last
trumpet. For the trumpet will sound, and the dead will
be raised incorruptible, and we shall be changed. For
this corruptible must put on incorruption, and this
mortal must put on immortality. So when this
corruptible has put on incorruption, and this mortal
has put on immortality, then shall be brought to pass
the saying that is written: "Death is swallowed up in
victory."* 1 Corinthians 15:50-54

Corruption refers to the process of death. To be
corruptible in this sense does not refer to moral

degeneration. It refers to physical degeneration. The process of generation and decay does not belong to the incorruptible. That which is free from physical corruption must escape all forms of generation and decay. That means that aging, wrinkles, acne, and disease have no place in that which is incorruptible. Not only death, but all of death's attendants are vanquished by the resurrection of the body.

The Intermediate State

The Bible does not teach two states of human life, but three. There is life as we know it on earth. There is the final state of our future resurrected bodies. And there is what happens to us between the moment of our deaths and the final resurrection.

Historically, Christian theology speaks of the intermediate state which refers to the continued personal existence of our souls in heaven until they are reclothed with a glorified body. In the intermediate state we will continue to exist, alive, as disembodied spirits.

Orthodox Christianity rejects the notion of soul sleep that has been made popular in some pockets of religion. The idea of soul sleep builds on the biblical use of the term "sleep" as a euphemism for death. It teaches that at death the departed souls of the saints remain in a kind of suspended animation, unconscious, and unaware of the passing of time until the great resurrection. It sees an analogy between soul sleep and the sleep experiences we have in this life (without dreams). When we sleep in this life we have the sensation of the suspension of time while we are unconscious.

The New Testament knows nothing of soul sleep. As

we have clearly seen, Paul describes the intermediate
state as better than this life, inasmuch as we move to
the immediate presence of Christ. It is difficult to
imagine how this state could be better than that which
we enjoy now if we remained unconscious in the
presence of Christ.

Of course there is the respite and cessation from
pain and turmoil that comes from sleep, but the
conscious fellowship with Christ we presently enjoy in
this life is not to be despised. There are times when we
long for unconscious slumber to gain relief from the
cares of this world, but the normal desire is to awaken
in order to resume conscious life. The great model of
Christian bliss is not found in the behavior of Rip Van
Winkle.

What glimpses the Bible does give to the
intermediate state strongly suggest a state of alert
consciousness. Though it is a parable that cannot be
forced too far, the parable of the rich man and Lazarus
suggests a keen conscious awareness of both men. The
parable involves a conversation between the rich man
and Abraham. The rich man, conscious of his torment,
cried out to Abraham for mercy. Abraham replied,

*Son, remember that in your lifetime you received your
good things, and likewise Lazarus evil things, but now
he is comforted and you are tormented. And besides
all this, between us and you there is a great gulf fixed,
so that those who want to pass from here to you
cannot, nor can those from there pass to us.*
Luke 16:25-26

Then the rich man pleads for the opportunity to
have a message sent to his brothers who are still alive,

that they may be warned about the place of torment
(vv. 27-28).

Though it is a parable, Jesus paints a picture of the
"bosom of Abraham" as an intermediate place of
conscious felicity and Hades as a place of conscious
torment. The scene is one that takes place obviously
prior to the great resurrection.

The vision of John recorded in the Book of
Revelation includes scenes of departed saints who
await the final state of glory:

When He opened the fifth seal, I saw under the altar
the souls of those who had been slain for the word of
God and for the testimony which they held. And they
cried with a loud voice, saying, "How long, O Lord,
holy and true, until You judge and avenge our blood
on those who dwell on earth?" And a white robe was
given to each of them; and it was said to them that
they should rest a little while longer, until both the
number of their fellow servants and their brethren,
who would be killed as they were, was completed.
Revelation 6:9-11

Here the souls of the martyrs are clearly in a state of
rest in their intermediate state. But this rest is not a
state of unconscious slumber. It is a conscious rest, a
rest in which they are capable of conversation.

Another crucial New Testament text that bears on
the issue of the intermediate state is found in Luke
23:43. Here Jesus speaks to the thief on the cross next
to Him. "Assuredly, I say to you, today you will be
with Me in Paradise."

In the original Greek text there is no punctuation.
No commas appear. The commas are supplied by the

translator. The debate about soul sleep centers on Jesus' use of the word *today*. The translator renders the sense of Jesus' words in this manner—*today* you shall be with Me. That is, the promise to the thief is that he will enjoy fellowship with Christ in paradise and that fellowship will begin on that very day.

Advocates of soul sleep use a different form of punctuation. They move the comma to a different point and render Jesus' statement in this manner: "I say to you today, you will be with Me in Paradise."

In this rendition the word *today* does not refer to the time when the thief will be with Jesus in Paradise. Rather it signifies the time when Jesus makes the promise of a reunion in the indefinite future. Though this rendition is grammatically possible it is not preferred either contextually or in strict literary terms. For Jesus to take the trouble to point out what time it is when He is speaking to the thief is to labor the obvious. There was no point in telling the thief that "today" was the day the two men were having a conversation. If they had a previous conversation in the past and Jesus had said, "Some day I'm going to tell you something very important, but today is not the right time"—And then later He makes His declaration, it would be appropriate to say, "All right, today is the day I'm going to tell you what I refused to reveal in the past. Today I say to you, some time in the future you will be with me in Paradise."

The statement becomes all the more problematic if we consider Jesus' physical condition at the time of the utterance. He was in the midst of the agony of crucifixion, when every word He uttered required a serious effort. It seems unlikely that Jesus would waste His dying breath to tell the thief that He was speaking to Him "today."

The prima facie interpretation would be to assume that the classical punctuation is correct. The word *today* takes on real significance if we understand Jesus to say, "I say to you, *today* you will be with Me in Paradise." The force of the words then mean, "On this very day when you are dying, on this day when you have every reason to abandon hope—on this, the last day of your earthly life—this very day will mark your entrance into a far better state than the one you are enduring at the moment. This is the day you enter Paradise."

This is the preferred rendition unless there is compelling biblical evidence to the contrary. No such evidence exists. Indeed, that believers enter immediately into the blessed intermediate state is the consistent and harmonious view of the rest of Scripture.

CHAPTER NINE

WHAT IS HEAVEN LIKE?

The most vivid and dramatic portrayal of heaven that
we can find in Scripture is at the end of the Revelation
of John. John was privileged to see, in the Spirit, a
spectacular vision of the future. The culmination of the
dramatic vision is found in the unveiling of the new
heaven and new earth.

*And I saw a new heaven and a new earth, for the first
heaven and the first earth had passed away. Also there
was no more sea.* Revelation 21:1

Here in capsule form we see the ultimate goal of the
suffering church, the culmination of God's entire plan

of the history of redemption. The future of creation is found in the manifestation of a new heaven and a new earth.

We are told that the first earth and the first heaven pass away. What does this mean? Interpreters are divided on this question. Some view the passing away of the original creation as an act of divine judgment on a fallen world. The old order is destroyed, annihilated by God's fury. Then the old is replaced by a new act of creation. Out of nothing God brings forth the new order.

A second view of the matter, and the one that I favor, is that the new order involves not a new creation out of nothing, but rather *renovation* of the old order. Its newness is marked by the work of God's redemption. The Scripture often speaks of the entire creation awaiting the final act of redemption. To destroy something completely and to replace it with something utterly new is not an act of redemption. To redeem something is to save that which is in imminent danger of being lost. The renovation may be radical. It may involve a violent conflagration of purging, but the purifying act ultimately redeems rather than annihilates. The new heaven and the new earth are purified. There is no room for evil in the new order. A hint of this is found in the somewhat cryptic words, "Also there was no more sea."

The Absence of the Chaotic Sea

For people who have a love for the seashore and all that it represents in terms of beauty and recreation, it may seem strange to contemplate a new earth without any sea. But to the ancient Jew it was a different matter. In Jewish literature the sea is often used as a symbolic image for something ominous, sinister, and threatening. Already in the Revelation of John we see the Antichrist Beast emerging from the sea. In ancient Semitic mythology there is frequent reference to the primordial sea monster that represents the shadowy chaos. The Babylonian goddess Tiamat is a case in point.

In Jewish thought it is the river, the stream, or the spring that functions as the positive symbol of goodness. This is natural in a desert habitat where the stream is life itself. If we look at a relief map of Palestine we see how crucial to the life of the land is the River Jordan. It cuts like a ribbon through the heart of an arid and parched land, connecting the Sea of Galilee in the north with the Dead Sea in the south.

The Mediterranean coast of western Palestine is marked by rocky shoals and jutting mountains. The ancient Hebrews did not develop a sea trade because the terrain was not suitable for much shipping. The sea represented trouble to them. It was from the Mediterranean that violent storms arose. We see this graphic imagery in Psalm 46:

God is our refuge and strength, a very present help in trouble. Therefore we will not fear, though the earth be removed, and though the mountains be carried into the midst of the sea; though its waters roar and be troubled, though the mountains shake with its swelling. Psalm 46:1-3

Note the immediate contrast with the following verse: "There is a river whose streams shall make glad the city of God" (v. 4).

I live in central Florida. Our area is sometimes described as the lightning capitol of America. The summer months bring severe electrical storms. My grandchildren are frequently frightened by what they call the "booming." The loud thunderclaps are not a part of what they would envision heaven to include.

But the Jews feared other problems from the sea besides turbulent storms. Their traditional archrivals, marauders who beset them countless times, were a seacoast nation. The Philistines came from the direction of the sea.

The Jew looked to a new world where all the evils symbolized by the sea would be absent. Heaven has water. Heaven has a river. Heaven has life-giving streams. But there is no sea there.

The Redeemed City

Then I, John, saw the holy city, New Jerusalem, coming down out of heaven from God, prepared as a bride adorned for her husband. Revelation 21:2

The zenith of the new order is seen in the arrival of the City of God, the redeemed Zion, the Jerusalem that descends from heaven.

The image of the city in Jewish literature is ambivalent. It oscillates between a negative and a positive image. On the one hand the Jewish people were historically seminomadic. They moved from grazing land to grazing land. They were a people who dwelt in tents. The God of Israel is the One who was first worshiped in a portable tent, a tabernacle.

Yet the people longed for stability, for a sense of

permanence. They rejoiced when the portable
tabernacle gave way to a majestic temple site under
the reign of David and Solomon. They were a people
who, like the patriarch Abraham,

sojourned in a land of promise as in a foreign country,
dwelling in tents with Isaac and Jacob, the heirs with
him of the same promise; for he waited for the city
which has foundations, whose builder and maker is
God. Hebrews 11:9-10

Christ is celebrated in the New Testament as the
great High Priest of the good things to come, "with the
greater and more perfect tabernacle not made with
hands, that is, not of this creation" (Hebrews 9:11).

On the other hand, the image of the city can be
negative when it represents man's arrogant attempt to
create a monument to himself. The city knows a place
of wickedness and corruption as we see in the history
of Sodom and Gomorrah. It is significant that the
author of Genesis mentions among the activities of the
first murderer, Cain, that he built a city:

Then Cain went out from the presence of the Lord
and dwelt in the land of Nod on the east of Eden. And
Cain knew his wife, and she conceived and bore Enoch.
And he built a city, and called the name of the city after
the name of his son—Enoch. Genesis 4:16-17

The city of Cain was unholy, as the cities of Sodom
and Gomorrah were unholy. It was Jerusalem that
became the focal point of Jewish future hope. Here, on
Mount Zion, was where God promised to dwell with
His people. It was here that the temple was built and

to which sacred pilgrimages were made. It was up to Jerusalem that the Messiah-king had to go to die.

The great holocaust of Israel took place in 70 A.D. when the Romans utterly destroyed the Holy City and the Jews were dispersed throughout the world. For centuries—even to this day—when the Jews celebrated the Passover they whispered their poignant hope to each other, "Next year in Jerusalem."

Israel was the bride of Yahweh, even as the church in the New Testament is called the bride of Christ. In John's vision the appearance of the New Jerusalem is likened to the spectacular appearance of the bride at the wedding hour. When the New Jerusalem appears, the city of man passes away, and the city of God is ushered in. The entrance of this city is heralded by a heavenly voice.

And I heard a loud voice from heaven saying, "Behold the tabernacle of God is with men, and He will dwell with them, and they shall be His people, and God Himself will be with them and be their God."
Revelation 21:3

The chief feature of the New Jerusalem is the *immediate presence* of God. God is in the midst of His people. He dwells with them. No longer is God seen as distant, remote from everyday experience. He pitches his tent in the midst of His people.

The closing words of Ezekiel's vision in the Old Testament capture the essence of the Holy City:

All the way around shall be eighteen thousand cubits; and the name of the city from that day shall be: THE LORD IS THERE. Ezekiel 48:35

When John penned the prologue to his Gospel, he spoke of the Logos, the Word of God who was in the beginning with God, and who was God.

And the Word became flesh and dwelt among us, and we beheld His glory, the glory as of the only begotten of the Father, full of grace and truth. John 1:14

When John speaks of the Incarnation he says that the Word "dwelt" among us. The word He uses literally means "pitched His tent" or "tabernacled." Jesus is called Emmanuel, meaning "God with us." The first visit of God Incarnate to Jerusalem was temporary. He came to Jerusalem and then He left Jerusalem. But He is a permanent resident of the New Jerusalem. He never takes His leave from the Holy City. There is no point of departure from that place.

The End of All Sorrow

And God will wipe away every tear from their eyes; there shall be no more death, nor sorrow, nor crying; and there shall be no more pain, for the former things have passed away. Revelation 21:4

When I was a child my mother always ministered to me tenderly when I was hurt. When tears spilled out of my eyes and I sobbed with uncontrollable spasms, my mother took her handkerchief and patted the tears from my cheeks. Often she would "kiss away the tears."

There are few more intimate human experiences than the physical act of wiping away another person's tears. It is a tactile act of compassion. It is a piercing form of nonverbal communication. It is the touch of consolation.

My mother dried my tears more than once. Her consolation worked for the moment and the sobbing subsided. But then I would get hurt again, and the tears would flow once more. My tear ducts still work. I still have the capacity to weep.

But when God wipes away tears, it is the end of all crying. John writes, "There shall be no more crying." Any tears shed in heaven could only be tears of joy. When God dries our eyes from all sorrowful weeping, the consolation will be permanent.

In heaven there will be no reason for mournful tears. Death will be no more. There will be no sorrow, no pain whatever. These things belong to the former things that shall pass away.

The New Jerusalem has no cemeteries. There is no morgue, no funeral parlor, no hospital, no painkilling drugs. These are the elements that attend the travail of this world. They will all pass away.

Then He who sat on the throne said, "Behold, I make all things new." And He said to me, "Write, for these words are true and faithful." Revelation 21:5

If anything sounds too good to be true, it is the announcement of the place where pain, sorrow, tears, and death are banished. The heart almost faints at the thought of it. We are almost afraid to think of it, lest we set ourselves up for a bitter disappointment. But the commanding voice from the imperial throne of God spoke decisively to John. "Write it down!" he ordered. "These words are true and faithful."

To call these words true means simply that they correspond to reality. They are not the vacuous promises of fantasy. That they are "faithful" means that they can be trusted without fear of disappointment.

And He said to me "It is done! I am the Alpha and the Omega, the Beginning and the End. I will give of the fountain of the water of life freely to him who thirsts."
Revelation 21:6

The Greek alphabet begins with the letter Alpha and ends with the letter Omega, corresponding to our A and Z. Christ reveals Himself as the Beginning and the End of all things. Again we hear the triumphant note of the victory of creation. There is no hint of an eternal cycle of meaningless repetition. There is a goal, a destiny for all of human history. The One who creates all things brings all things to a meaningful conclusion. Vanity and futility are exiled in the light of One who is Alpha and Omega.

The One who is the Author and the Finisher of our faith promises satisfied refreshment to all who are thirsty. The powerful image of thirst appears frequently in the Scriptures. The psalmist wrote:

As the deer pants for the water brooks, so pants my soul for You, O God. My soul thirsts for God, for the living God. Psalm 42:1-2

The human longing for God is likened to the deer whose tongue hangs out in search for water. The emotion is intense; the thirst is a driving one. It is to this type of person, one who has a passionate yearning for God that Christ uttered His benediction: "Blessed are those who hunger and thirst for righteousness, for they shall be filled" (Matthew 5:6).

Jesus' words are reminiscent of His conversation with the Samaritan woman at the well:

If you knew the gift of God, and who it is who says to you, "Give Me a drink," you would have asked Him, and He would have given you living water. . . . Whoever drinks of the water that I shall give him will never thirst. But the water that I shall give him will become in him a fountain of water springing up into everlasting life. John 4:10-14

These promises reach a crescendo with the words of Jesus: "It is done!" He has accomplished His mission and the future victory is assured.

He who overcomes shall inherit all things, and I will be his God and he shall be My son. But the cowardly, unbelieving, abominable, murderers, sexually immoral, sorcerers, idolaters, and all liars shall have their part in the lake which burns with fire and brimstone, which is the second death. Revelation 21:7-8

This passage sounds an ominous note of warning. It refers to the final act of Christ's judgment. To those who are faithful comes the promise of full participation in Christ's inheritance. We are called joint-heirs with Christ when we are adopted into the family of God. But those who persist in their opposition to Christ, those who are allied with the Antichrist, are excluded from the felicity of heaven and are consigned to the lake of fire. The catalog of sins mentioned (lying, idolatry, etc.) represent a capsule summary of the characteristics of the followers of the Antichrist who obstinately refuse to show loyalty to Christ.

The Radiance of the Holy City

Then one of the seven angels who had the seven bowls filled with the seven last plagues came to me and talked with me, saying, "Come, I will show you the bride, the Lamb's wife."

And He carried me away in the Spirit to a great and high mountain, and showed me the great city, the holy Jerusalem, descending out of heaven from God, having the glory of God. And her light was like a most precious stone, like a jasper stone, clear as crystal.
Revelation 21:10-11

The same angel who had earlier (chapter 17) shown John a vision of the great harlot, the city of Babylon, now carries him away to see the ultimate city of contrast. The Holy City is bathed in the refulgent glory of God. It radiates in breathtaking brilliance. Its light is likened to a jasper stone. Earlier in Revelation the divine appearance on the throne was described in these words: "And He who sat there was like a jasper and a sardius stone in appearance" (Revelation 4:3).

Jasper stones may vary in appearance from yellow to red to green. They may also be translucent. Sardius was red. The city appears reflecting the shekinah glory of God, transparent and fiery red, as the light.

Also she had a great and high wall with twelve gates, and twelve angels at the gates, and names written on them, which are the names of the twelve tribes of the

*children of Israel; three gates on the east, three gates
on the north, three gates on the south, and three gates
on the west.* Revelation 21:12-13

In the ancient world the strength and majesty of a
city was measured by its wall. The wall not only
marked the city's boundaries, but was a vital element
of protection against enemy attack. Ancient warfare
necessarily involved the siege and the catapult. Today
visitors to the old city of Jerusalem are immediately
impressed by the wall that surrounds it. Built of great
Herodian stones, the wall of Jerusalem reaches
seventy-five feet high. As staggering as this site is to
the modern visitor, it is rendered even more
remarkable that the erosion of time has hidden
another seventy-five feet that is now underground.

The wall of the earthly Jerusalem pales in
comparison to that of the heavenly Jerusalem. This
wall is great and high, indicating the total security of
those who dwell within. It affords an impregnable
barrier to any who would try to enter without the
invitation of God. Yet there is access through the
twelve gates named for the twelve tribes of Israel.
Salvation is of the Jews. The root of redemptive
history is planted upon the Jewish nation. But the new
Jerusalem has gates for people from all nations to
enter. Though it honors its original nation, Israel, it is
a place that all who desire to dwell with the Lamb may
enter.

*Now the wall of the city had twelve foundations, and
on them were the names of the twelve apostles of the
Lamb.* Revelation 21:14

We sing of the church's one foundation being Jesus. In the New Testament imagery, however, the symbol most often used for Christ is that of the cornerstone. No other foundation can be laid except that which is laid in Christ. And the image of the foundation is also used for the apostles:

Having been built on the foundation of the apostles and prophets, Jesus Christ Himself being the Chief cornerstone. Ephesians 2:20

It is significant that the wall rests not on one foundation, but on twelve. The symmetry here of twelve gates and twelve foundations symbolizing the twelve tribes of Israel and the twelve apostles show the unity of the Old and New Testaments and the complete inclusion of the total people of God.

And he who talked with me had a gold reed to measure the city, its gates, and its wall. And the city is laid out as a square, and its length is as great as its breadth. And he measured the city with the reed: twelve thousand furlongs. Its length, breadth, and height are equal. Then he measured its wall; one hundred and forty four cubits, according to the measure of a man, that is, of an angel. Revelation 21:15-17

The Holy City is measured by a golden instrument. The measurements reveal the perfect symmetry of the city. There are no stray lines, nothing out of balance. The City of God is perfectly plumb. We note that the city is a cube. The cube structure recalls the dimensions of the holy of holies in the Old Testament.

(See 1 Kings 6:20.) Perhaps this explains a feature of the New Jerusalem that surely would have been surprising to Jews, namely that the city has no temple in it. The whole city is a temple, permeated by the presence of God.

The city measures 1500 miles. The sum is symbolic. It represents the unit of the furlong multiplied by twelve. It is extended indefinitely. Imagine a city that extended in scope from about New York to Denver.

The measurements of the wall are also amazing. The 144 cubits again represents the multiple of twelve. A cubit was originally measured as the length from a man's fingertip to his elbow. Some have estimated the wall at 216 feet. But we note that it is the cubit as measured by an angel that is used here.

And the construction of its wall was of jasper; and the city was pure gold, like clear glass. Revelation 21:8

Recently someone gave me a tape that rehearsed the events that took place in the year of my birth, 1939. One of the events mentioned was the building of the Hearst mansion that was the most elaborate and expensive private dwelling built in America. The mansion included over a hundred rooms and cost $30 million in 1939. The gold fixtures in it were spectacular. But the Hearst mansion is a doghouse compared to the New Jerusalem.

We cannot fathom a city of pure gold that is like clear glass. We recall that Solomon's temple featured a lavish degree of gold plate. But the New City is not mere gold plate. It is pure gold that radiates the beauty of God's holiness.

*And the foundations of the wall of the city were
adorned with all kinds of precious stones: the first
foundation was jasper, the second sapphire, the third
chalcedony, the fourth emerald, the fifth sardonyx, the
sixth sardius, the seventh chrysolite, the eighth beryl,
the ninth topaz, the tenth chrysoprase, the eleventh
jacinth, and the twelfth amethyst.* Revelation 21:19-20

The precious jewels found in the city's foundation
bring to mind the jewels that adorned the breastplate
of the high priest of Israel. (See Exodus 28:15ff.) Some
have seen in them a subtle rejection of pagan religion
as he lists them in reverse order of how they function
in zodiac astrology. The true reality that is distorted in
pagan religion is found in the city of God.

*And the twelve gates were twelve pearls: each
individual gate was of one pearl, and the street of the
city was pure gold, like transparent glass.*
Revelation 21:21

Here is the text that provides the popular conception
of heaven with "pearly gates" and the streets of gold.
The verse recalls a prophecy found in Isaiah 54:12.
The rabbis in antiquity sometimes took Isaiah's
prophecy literally and looked forward to a time when
Jerusalem would have pearls thirty cubits wide and
twenty cubits high with an opening in them of ten by
twenty cubits. (Imagine the size of the oysters that
would produce such pearls.)

I was born and raised in Pittsburgh. Pittsburgh is a
lovely city, far more beautiful than the popular image
of a city blanketed by soot and smog from belching

steel mills. The city has been on the cutting edge of urban renewal and a model for urban renaissance. Pittsburgh's problem is not the smoke stacks of the steel mills. (Most of them are now idle.) The perennial problem that plagues the city fathers involves the notorious potholes in the streets. Late winter brings a constant flux of freeze and thaw that quickly destroys the surfaces of the roads. There are legends of Volkswagens being lost forever in the cavernous chuckholes in the road.

There are no potholes in the heavenly city. There are no road taxes necessary for constant maintenance. The streets are paved with crystal clear gold that never needs to be resurfaced.

These graphic images are most probably symbolic of the glory that will be present in heaven, though I shrink from being dogmatic about it. We ought not to put it past God that He may produce a city exactly as John envisioned it.

The City without a Temple

But I saw no temple in it, for the Lord God Almighty and the Lamb are its temple. Revelation 21:22

This verse would have been shocking to contemporary Jews who read it. A New Jerusalem with no temple was utterly inconceivable to them. Their future hope centered on the ultimate magnificence of the temple. Jesus' enemies were infuriated at His predictions of the destruction of the temple of Jerusalem (which took place in 70 A.D.).

When the Jews asked Jesus for a sign He answered by saying:

"Destroy this temple, and in three days I will raise it up." Then the Jews said, "It has taken forty-six years to build this temple, and will you raise it up in three days?" But He was speaking of the temple of His body. Therefore, when He had risen from the dead, His disciples remembered that He had said this to them; and they believed the Scripture and the word which Jesus had said. John 2:19-22

The temple is replaced by the immediate presence of God the Father and the Lamb, God the Son. The risen Christ is the "meeting place" between God and man. He is the Mediator of His people.

And the city had no need of the sun or of the moon to shine in it, for the glory of God illuminated it, and the Lamb is its light. Revelation 21:23

Again the words of Revelation echo the Old Testament prophecy of Isaiah:

The sun shall no longer be your light by day, nor for brightness shall the moon give light to you; but the LORD *will be to you an everlasting light, and your God your glory.* Isaiah 60:19

Christ declared that He was the "light of the world" (John 8:12). His resurrection splendor, along with the dazzling glory of God, will dwarf the lesser luminaries of the sun and the moon.

*And the nations of those who are saved shall walk in
its light, and the kings of the earth bring their glory
and honor into it. Its gates shall not be shut at all by
day (there shall be no night there). And they shall
bring the glory and the honor of the nations into it.
But there shall by no means enter it anything that
defiles, or causes an abomination or a lie, but only
those who are written in the Lamb's book of life.*
Revelation 21:24-27

The Holy City is a place where the people from all
nations will flock to render tribute to the Messiah
King. Earthly kings who are numbered among the
redeemed will hasten to bring their own glory, riches,
and honor to lay them at the feet of the Lamb. Just as
the ancient Magi journeyed far to offer gifts to the
Christ child, so in the future there will be a much more
spectacular visitation of kings and princes to the
throne of Christ. Then the nations will gather for
worship of the King of Kings. The gates will always
stand open. There will be no threat of nightfall, for
not a moment passes when shadows can obscure in the
constant splendor of the light of His presence.

Though the gates remain open, nothing that brings
defilement can pass through them. Entrance is barred
to any whose names are not written in the Lamb's
Book of Life. It is the Lamb's city and is open to all,
but only all who are His.

*And he showed me a pure river of water of life, clear
as crystal, proceeding from the throne of God and of
the Lamb. In the middle of its street, and on either
side of the river, was the tree of life, which bore twelve
fruits, each tree yielding its fruit every month. And the*

leaves of the tree were for the healing of the nations.
Revelation 22:1-2

This scene recalls some of the elements of the
Garden of Eden. We tend to think of heaven as the
restoration of the Paradise that was lost in the Fall.
But heaven is far more than a simple restoration of the
original order of things. The future Paradise far
exceeds the felicity that was enjoyed in the pristine
Eden.

The scene also resembles the prophecy of Ezekiel:

Then he said to me: "This water flows toward the
eastern region, goes down into the valley, and enters
the sea. When it reaches the sea, its waters are healed.
And it shall be that every living thing that moves,
wherever the rivers go, will live . . . and everything
will live wherever the river goes. . . . Along the bank
of the river, on this side and that, will grow all kinds
of trees used for food; their leaves will not wither, and
their fruit will not fail. They will bear fruit every
month, because their water flows from the sanctuary.
Their fruit will be for food, and their leaves for
medicine." Ezekiel 47:7-12

In Ezekiel's vision the river flows from the temple.
In John's vision it is not the temple, but Christ
Himself, the Abiding Temple, who is the Source of the
healing water.

The Removal of the Curse

In John's vision it is difficult to determine whether he
saw one tree of life with branches on both sides of the

river or two separate trees of life. In either case the tree stands for the new order of life that will be present. The annual cycle of the seasons with birth in spring and death in winter is ended. The trees bear fresh fruit every month. Their leaves do not decay and die. The curse of the earth is over. No more thorns or briars are found in nature. There can be no drought to threaten the harvest.

The leaves of the tree are therapeutic. They contain the balm of healing for the wounds of the nations. John does not specify what maladies are in need of healing. Perhaps he has in mind the normal pain of nature that is removed. Or he could have in mind the healing of the wounds inflicted by the Antichrist.

And there shall be no more curse, but the throne of God, and of the Lamb shall be in it, and His servants shall serve Him. Revelation 22:3

The end of the curse signals the full consummation of divine redemption. The idea of the curse hearkens back to the fall of mankind. The curse is God's judgment upon disobedience. In the original fall God cursed the Serpent who beguiled Eve. He afflicted woman with pain in childbearing and man with the added burdens of his toil. The ground was cursed with thorns.

The curse motif appears again dramatically when God makes his covenant with Israel.

Behold, I set before you today a blessing and a curse: the blessing, if you obey the commandments of the Lord *your God which I command you today; and the curse, if you do not obey the commandments of the* Lord *your God.* Deuteronomy 11:26-28

The curse means far more than the loss of positive blessings. Ultimately it involves being cut off from the presence of God. When Christ was crucified and "forsaken" by the Father, He was cut off from the divine presence. The lights went out, and Jesus was plunged into an abysmal darkness.

The curse means that we cannot see the face of God in this world. It means that we experience a certain measure of the absence of God. But in John's vision when the curse is removed two things stand out immediately: First is the clear presence of God and the Lamb. Second is the willing service rendered by His people. This stands in bold contrast to the situation that brought on the curse in the first place. The curse fell because of disobedience. When the curse is gone there is no more disobedience. The curse and its cause, sin, are absent from heaven.

The Beatific Vision

They shall see His face, and His name shall be on their foreheads. Revelation 22:4

Here is the supreme hope of heaven. It describes what the theologians call the *beatific vision*. The beatific vision is a sight that provokes instant and profound joy. It is the blessedness and felicity for which everyone was created. Here the empty void that haunts the human soul is filled at last.

"They shall see His face." There is no more difficult problem that attends the life of faith than that we are called to serve and worship a God who is utterly invisible to us. At no point is the adage "out of sight out of mind" more keenly felt than in the object of our affections. We want to bathe our eyes in the majesty of His glory. We want Him to lift up the light of His countenance upon us. We yearn for Him to cause His face to shine upon us.

Even in the Old Testament narratives of divine appearances to human beings we have the record of what, at best, may be called *theophanies.* A theophany is a visible manifestation of the invisible God. Moses sees a bush that burns but is not consumed. The children of Israel behold the pillar of cloud. These theophanies still maintain a veil over the face of God.

In the First Letter of John, the apostle writes,

Behold what manner of love the Father has bestowed on us, that we should be called the children of God! Therefore the world does not know us, because it did not know Him. Beloved, now we are children of God; and it has not yet been revealed what we shall be, but we know that when He is revealed, we shall be like Him, for we shall see Him as He is. 1 John 3:1-2

John introduces this theme of the beatific vision with an expression of apostolic astonishment. He declares his profound amazement that the likes of us can be called the children of God. The bestowing of this privilege of adopted sonship reflects a "manner" or kind of love that defies all normal categories. It is a transcendent manner of love that moves the Father to call us His children. We are categorically unworthy of such a title. The grounds for it cannot be found in any merit in us. The only possible explanation for our being called the children of God must rest in the extraordinary love that only God is capable of displaying.

John goes on to confess that it has not yet been revealed what we shall be. The mirror is still dark. The future is still cloudy. But a few hints are given that are enough to set our souls on fire. One thing we know for sure; one glimpse of light penetrates the darkness of the mirror. *We shall be like Him.*

It is full of irony that as creatures of God we were made in His image. The intent of God's creation of the human race was that we should mirror and reflect the very character of God. But in the reality of our fallenness that image has been besmirched. As images of God we become lying images. The image is distorted. There is nothing more characteristic of human beings than that we sin. In our sin we demonstrate precisely what God is *not* like. There is no shadow of evil in the character of God.

When sin is altogether removed from us then we shall be authentic images of our God. We shall be like Him.

John doesn't tell us the exact order of events. Is it that we will first be made pure so that it becomes possible to see God; or is it that the naked sight of the unveiled God will be the experience that instantly purifies us? I am not sure which it is, but I suspect that it is the former.

The promise of Jesus in the Beatitudes is this: "Blessed are the pure in heart, for they shall see God" (Matthew 5:8).

The absolute prerequisite for beholding the face of God is purity of heart. The reason why God is invisible to mortal men is because no mortal is pure in heart. The problem is not with our eyes; it is with our hearts. Only when we are glorified in heaven will we be qualified to see God. Therefore, I suppose that

before we will "see Him as He is," the residue of
defilement will first be utterly cleansed from our
hearts.

There is a scene in the Hollywood version of Lew
Wallace's *Ben-Hur* that captures something of the
poignancy of the vision of Christ. Ben-Hur is by a
well, and he is filthy, stooped in the dirt, and overcome
with a fierce thirst. The camera focuses on Ben-Hur's
face. His countenance is twisted in misery. Then the
shadow of a man crosses his visage. We do not see the
man. The camera remains fixed on Ben-Hur's face.
The man offers him water. As Ben-Hur lifts his
wretched face to behold the merciful stranger, we see a
sudden radiance transform his face. We know
instantly, by the radical change of his countenance,
that when he lifts his head he looks directly into the
face of Christ.

That is the ultimate hope of the Christian. When we
behold the face of God all memories of pain and
sufferings will vanish. Our total souls shall be healed.

God will put His name upon our foreheads. The
number of the Antichrist will not be there. We will be
marked with an indelible name that will identify us
forever as the sons and daughters of God.

*And there shall be no night there: they need no lamp
nor light of the sun, for the Lord God gives them
light. And they shall reign forever and ever. Then he
said to me, "These words are faithful and true."*
Revelation 22:5-6a

These words are the capstone of John's vision into
the secret chambers of heaven. Again he emphasizes
the banishment of all darkness. The refulgent glory of

God will bathe His people in light forever. Those who are His will receive their full inheritance. They will hear Him say: "Come, My beloved, inherit the kingdom which has been prepared for you from the beginning of time."

It is this promise, a promise certified by the heavenly declaration, "These words are faithful and true" that removes all doubt about our present pain and suffering. It is this promise that verifies the apostolic comparison that the afflictions we endure in this life are not even worthy to be compared with the glory God has stored up for us in heaven. It is this promise that is sealed by divine oath that our suffering is never, never, never in vain.

CONCLUSION

In his Letter to the Ephesians, Paul expressed the deep sentiments of his heart concerning believers:

Therefore I also, after I heard of your faith in the Lord Jesus and your love for all the saints, do not cease to give thanks for you, making mention of you in my prayers: that the God of our Lord Jesus Christ, the Father of glory, may give to you the Spirit of wisdom and revelation in the knowledge of Him, the eyes of your understanding being enlightened; that you may know what is the hope of His calling, what are the riches of the glory of His inheritance in the saints, and what is the exceeding greatness of His power toward us who believe, according to the working of His mighty power. Ephesians 1:15-10

In this expression of pastoral desire, Paul refers to all three of the great Christian virtues—faith, love, and hope. He exudes joy over hearing of the faith of the saints that shows itself in love. But the focus of his prayer is that the Spirit of God will so illumine the minds of believers with divine wisdom that we will come to a full appreciation of hope. He speaks here of the hope of His calling.

The divine vocation to us is not ultimately or finally to suffering, but to hope that goes far beyond suffering. It is the hope of our future inheritance with Christ.

This hope is no mere wish or idle longing of the soul. It is a hope that is rooted in the exceedingly great power of God. It is a hope that cannot fail. It is a hope that will never leave one who embraces it either ashamed or disappointed.

Hope beyond suffering is the legacy of Christ. It is the promise of God to all who put their trust in Him.

APPENDIX A:
QUESTIONS AND ANSWERS ON DEATH AND THE AFTERLIFE

How would you counsel Christians who are suffering with illness or old age infirmity who would rather be in heaven than to stay here?

First, I would commend such people for their preference. They are certainly in good company. Frequently this sentiment is expressed by biblical heroes and heroines. We remember the aged Simeon who, after waiting years to behold the Messiah, finally was blessed to see the Christ child in the temple. He took the baby Jesus in his arms and spoke the poem known as the *Nunc Dimittis:* "Lord, now You are letting Your servant depart in peace, according to Your word; for my eyes have seen Your salvation" (Luke 2:29-30).

Job, in the midst of his great pain, begged God for the release of death: "Oh, that I might have my request that God would grant me the thing I long for! That it would please God to crush me, that He would loose His hand and cut me off!" (Job 6:8-9). Moses and Jeremiah, among others, made the same plea.

I once heard a man describing the throes of seasickness by saying, "First, I was afraid I was going to die, and then I was afraid I wouldn't." What he uttered in jest is a sober reality for many who are afflicted.

Recently Billy Graham was quoted publicly as saying that he was tired and longed to go home and be with Christ. Dr. Graham's remarks echoed those of the Apostle Paul when he wrote

For to me, to live is Christ, and to die is gain. But if I live on in the flesh, this will mean fruit from my labor; yet what I shall choose I cannot tell. For I am hard pressed between the two, having a desire to depart and be with Christ, which is far better. Nevertheless to remain in the flesh is more needful for you.
Philippians 1:21-24

Paul was willing to continue his ministry on earth, but his clear preference was to die and be with Christ.

There are two basic reasons why Christians at times long for death. The first is to fulfill our deep longing to arrive at our spiritual destination. The pilgrimage of our souls is not finished until we enter into our rest. The second reason is obviously motivated by the desire for relief from affliction.

Søren Kierkegaard once wrote that one of the most anguishing experiences of life is to want to die and not be allowed to. Suicide is not permitted by God. The time of our death is in God's hands. We must not take steps to hasten the moment of our departure. God is the author of life and is sovereign over both life and death. We may pray for our own death, but the request may be granted by God and God alone.

What about suicide? What happens to those who commit suicide?

Historically the church has taken a dim view of suicide for reasons mentioned above. However, we are left with the fact that many people do, in fact, kill themselves.

I was once asked on a television talk show if people who committed suicide could go to heaven. I answered with a simple, "Yes." My answer caused the switchboard lights to glow like a Christmas tree. The host was shocked by my response.

I explained that suicide is nowhere identified as an unforgivable sin. We do not know with any degree of certainty what is going through a person's mind at the moment of suicide. It is possible that suicide is an act of pure unbelief, a succumbing to total despair that indicates the absence of any faith in God. On the other hand, it may be the sign of temporary or prolonged mental illness. It may result from a sudden wave of severe depression. (Such depression can in some cases be brought on by organic causes or by unintentional use of certain medication.)

One psychiatrist remarked that the vast majority of people who commit suicide would not have done so had they waited twenty-four hours. Such an observation is conjecture, but it is conjecture based upon numerous interviews of persons who made serious attempts at suicide but failed and consequently recovered.

The point is that people commit suicide for a wide variety of reasons. The complexity of the thinking process of a person at the moment of suicide is known comprehensively by God. God takes all mitigating circumstances into account when he renders his judgment on any person.

Though we must seek to discourage people from suicide, we leave those who have done it to the mercy of God.

How do you explain the out-of-body, "tunnel-like" experiences that many people have reported after being revived from death?
I can't offer a full explanation of the so-called Kubler-Ross phenomenon. There has been a significant amount of research on this, but the results are, at best, speculative. I've heard reports claiming that as many as 50 percent of those who have suffered clinical death and have been resuscitated through CPR or other means report some strange experience. Some report the sensation of looking down from the ceiling and seeing their own body lying in the bed while doctors or nurses were making administrations. Some have reported moving through a vast tunnel that is bathed in a brilliant light.

Most of these reports have been of a positive nature. Others, however, have reported frightening and ominous experiences that gave them pause about what might be awaiting them beyond the veil.

Religious interpretations of these sensations are

complicated by the fact that often the same positive experiences are reported by believers and unbelievers alike.

Various explanations for the phenomenon have been offered. One involves a type of hallucination potential brought on by medication, or short circuits in the brain similar to the explanation often rendered for *déjà vu* experiences. (One theory of the *déjà vu* is that impulses to the brain trigger a response that creates a feeling of memory, though it is not actual memory. That is, while we are undergoing an experience we have an eerie feeling that we have already lived this experience once before. The *déjà vu* has elements, however, that remain mysterious. For example, there are cases where we "know" what a person is going to say or do in a situation before it happens.)

Another explanation is based on the biblical affirmation of life after death. As Christians we believe that the soul survives death. There is a continuity of personal existence after the cessation of physical life. Whether we're good or bad, redeemed or unredeemed, we continue the life of the soul.

I'm fascinated by these reports and look forward to future scientific analysis of them. I keep before me, however, the parable of the rich man and Lazarus, in which the warning is uttered, "If they do not hear Moses and the prophets, neither will they be persuaded though one rise from the dead" (Luke 16:31).

Can suffering in general, rather than persecution for the name of Christ, be called sharing the suffering of Christ?
I think that in some cases it can. If our suffering is done in faith, if we place our trust in God while we are

suffering, then we are emulating the trust Jesus had in the Father. Certainly there is a special promise given to those who suffer unjustly. Those who are persecuted for righteousness sake have a host of biblical promises to comfort them.

But what if a person is suffering from an illness or some tragedy that is not a result of persecution? Here placing one's trust in God in the midst of affliction is a virtue that is not without reward. It still involves a kind of imitation of Christ. It does not involve redemptive merit, but God is surely honored and pleased when his children keep the faith in the midst of suffering. In this we follow the example of Christ.

Indeed, we may also suffer as a just consequence for our sins. In this sense we are not imitating Christ, yet even here it is possible to honor God. God was honored when the thief on the cross acknowledged that he deserved the punishment he was experiencing. He did not add blasphemy or slandering of God to the sins he was already guilty of.

What happens to animals when they die?

This is not a frivolous question. We know that people get very attached to animals, particularly their household pets. The little girl with her kitten, the man and his dog, all exhibit the very human affection that passes between humans and animals.

Traditionally many have been persuaded that there is no future life for animals. The Bible does not explicitly teach that animals go to heaven. One of the key arguments against the idea that animals do not survive the grave is the conviction that animals do not have souls. Many are convinced that the distinctive aspect that divides humans from animals is that humans have souls and animals do not. Some locate the *image of God* in man in the soul.

Likewise it is assumed that animals cannot think as we do. Their responses are explained by *instinct* rather than lower forms of *cognition*. However, the term *instinct* is a study in ambiguity. When does instinct become thought? Animals can display what we call emotion. They surely respond to external stimuli.

The Bible doesn't say that animals think. The Bible doesn't say that animals have souls. But neither does the Bible deny these things. To be sure the Bible says the ox knows his master's crib. Here "knowledge" is assigned to an animal. However, the passage could be interpreted metaphorically or poetically, so we remain uncertain.

One thing we are sure of: Biblically, redemption is spelled out in cosmic terms. Just as the whole creation was plunged into ruin by the fall of man, so the whole creation groans together awaiting redemption.

For the earnest expectation of the creation eagerly waits for the revealing of the sons of God. For the creation was subjected to futility, not willingly, but because of Him who subjected it in hope; because the creation itself also will be delivered from the bondage of corruption into the glorious liberty of the children of God. Romans 8:19-21.

Images of heaven and future redemption include animals. The lamb, the lion, the wolf are all mentioned. Again, these images may only be metaphorically illustrative. But coupled with the promise of cosmic redemption they lend some real hope to the future redemption of man's animal companions.

Is it wrong to try to avoid suffering?

There have been times in church history that suffering was looked upon as such a virtue that people went out of their way to experience it. The ancient heresy of Manichaeism, which focused on releasing the soul from the evil flesh, has had a powerful influence upon the church. Rigorous acts of asceticism, including bizarre forms of self-flagellation, have been seen as ways of accruing merit in the sight of God. But suffering merely for the sake of suffering has no particular virtue. The quest for suffering may indicate a psychological disorder such as masochism. It may also indicate an attempt at self-justification whereby a person, out of pride, wants to atone for his own sins rather than to receive the grace of forgiveness.

There is no reason to seek suffering. Nor is there anything wrong in trying to avoid it unless avoiding it purposely involves a betrayal of Christ. The early martyrs could have avoided the lions if they repudiated Christ. Here was an instance whereby the avoidance of suffering would have been sin. (Such examples are not limited to the early church. In many situations in the contemporary world, notably in Marxist countries, Christians choose—and in some cases do not choose—to suffer for Christ.)

We seek to avoid suffering when we buy food to eat and use medicine to heal our diseases. This is not sin, but prudence. God calls us to take care of ourselves in the stewardship of both body and soul.

We conclude that the avoidance of suffering may

either be virtue or sin, depending upon the
circumstances involved.

When a baby dies or is aborted, where does its soul go?

The way this question is worded indicates a certain
ambiguity about the relationship between abortion
and death. If life begins at conception, then abortion is
a type of death. If life does not begin until birth, then
obviously abortion does not involve death. The
classical view of this is that life begins at conception. If
that is so then the question of infant death and
prenatal death involve the same answer.

Any time a human being dies before reaching the age
of accountability (which varies according to mental
capacity), we must look to special provisions of God's
mercy. Most churches believe that there is such a
special provision in the mercy of God. This view does
not involve an assumption of innocence in infants.
David declared that he was both born in sin and
conceived in sin. By this he was obviously referring to
the biblical notion of original sin. Original sin does not
refer to the first sin of Adam and Eve, but to the result
of that initial transgression. Original sin refers to the
condition of our fallenness that affects all human
beings. We are not sinners because we sin, but we sin
because we are sinners. That is, we sin because we are
born with a sinful nature.

Though infants are not guilty of actual sin, they are
tainted with original sin. That is why we insist that the
salvation of infants depends not on their presumed
innocence, but upon God's grace.

My particular church believes that the children of
believers who die in infancy go to heaven by the

special grace of God. What happens to the children of unbelievers is left to the realm of mystery. There may also be a special provision of God's grace for them as well. We can certainly hope for that.

Even though we hope for such grace, there is little specific biblical teaching on the matter. Jesus' words, "Let the little children come to Me; for of such is the kingdom of heaven" (Matthew 19:14), give us some consolation, but do not offer a categorical promise of infant salvation.

When the son of David and Bathsheba was taken by God, David lamented, "While the child was still alive, I fasted and wept; for I said, 'Who can tell whether the LORD will be gracious to me, that the child may live?' But now he is dead; why should I fast? Can I bring him back again? I shall go to him, but he shall not return to me" (2 Samuel 12:22-23).

Here David declares his confidence that "I shall go to him." It is a thinly veiled reference to his hope of future reunion with his son. This hope of future reunion is a glorious hope that abides in all parents who have lost their children. It is a hope that is buttressed by the New Testament teaching on the resurrection.

Where does free will play a role in suffering? For example, if a man smokes and then dies from cancer, is his suffering a call from God as a vocation? Is it a divine judgment? Or is it a result of the man taking his chances?

The question lists three possible explanations for the suffering described. We can eliminate one of them altogether. If God is sovereign, then nothing happens purely by chance. A chance event would be totally outside of the sovereign will of God. If any such events were outside the sovereign will of God then it would be a contradiction in terms to call God sovereign. As I've written elsewhere, if there is one maverick molecule in the universe running around free of God's sovereignty then there is no guarantee that any promise God has ever made will come to pass. That one molecule may be the very thing that disrupts God's eternal plan. Here even the best laid plans not of mice and men but of the Creator himself, might go astray.

If God is not sovereign, then God is not God. A non-sovereign God is no God at all. A non-sovereign God would be like a titular king who reigns but doesn't rule. To be sure, men have free will but our free will is limited. It is always limited by God's free will. God's free will is a sovereign free will. Our free will is a subordinate free will.

When I speak of suffering being a vocation I have in mind that God is sovereign over everything that happens to us. That does not cancel out our free will and responsibility.

The question remains, is the suffering mentioned the result of God's vocation or God's judgment? Here we face a false dilemma. This need not be an either/or situation. God's call to suffer may at the same time be an act of judgment.

We remember the nocturnal call that came to Samuel when he served under Eli. God revealed to Samuel that he was going to bring his holy judgment upon the house of Eli. Eli then begged Samuel to tell him what God revealed.

"What is the thing that the Lord *has said to you?*
Please do not hide it from me. God do so to you, and
more also, if you hide anything from me of all the
things that He said to you." Then Samuel told him
everything, and hid nothing from him. And he said, "It
is the Lord. *Let Him do what seems good to Him."*
1 Samuel 3:17-18

Eli recognized the judgment of God. He recognized
the justice of it. He acquiesced to it. Here he accepted
a vocation, a call to himself to bear the chastisement in
suffering.

Likewise when Nathan told David that David had
sinned, David repented. David's life was spared, but
his son's was not.

Then David said to Nathan, "I have sinned against the
Lord." *And Nathan said to David, "The* Lord *also*
has put away your sin; you shall not die. However,
because by this deed you have given great occasion
to the enemies of the Lord *to blaspheme, the child*
also who is born to you shall surely die."
2 Samuel 12:13-14

The record reports that David then pleaded with
God for the child. He fasted and prayed. But God said
no. On the seventh day the child died. What was
David's response? "So David arose from the ground,
washed and anointed himself, and changed his clothes;
and he went into the house of the Lord and
worshiped" (2 Samuel 12:20).

David worshiped God in the midst of his suffering.
Indeed, he knew he was suffering under the corrective

judgment of God. David answered the call of God righteously.

David's response echoes that of Job when Job declared, "Naked I came from my mother's womb, and naked shall I return there. The LORD gave, and the LORD has taken away; blessed be the name of the LORD" (Job 1:21).

APPENDIX B:
CONTACTING THE DEAD

The speculations of men like Plato and Kant provide a
measure of comfort concerning the question of life
after death. Their work shows that at best the idea of
continued personal existence beyond the grave is not
repugnant to reason or nature. Their arguments give
us corroborative support for the hope we hold so dear.
Yet their arguments remain speculative. We are left
with the uneasy feelings that perhaps reality is not as
rational as Plato would like it to be nor nature as just
as Kant hoped it to be.

We long for concrete, tangible proof that life
continues after death. We want the assurance that

someone has gone beyond and has come back, or at least has given us a message from the other side.

The Forbidden Realm: Spiritualism

The practice of necromancy, commonly called *spiritualism*, demonstrates mankind's profound desire to gain firsthand information from the other side. The séance of the spiritualist promises such information via the trappings of medium communication, table rappings, and the appearance of ghostly shapes of ectoplasm.

Though a tiny segment of the population gives credence to the practice of medium consultations, for the most part spiritualism is consigned to the realm of fraudulent occultism. Some see spiritualism as out and out hoax-mongering, while others view it as a manifestation of the real but demonic.

I was once an unwitting participant in a séance. I had gone to a church to deliver a lecture series and was invited to a prayer meeting after the opening service. A group of Christians gathered in a home, ostensibly for the purpose of prayer. The lights were turned off, and the leader began beseeching the Holy Spirit of God to empower contact with departed friends and relatives. To my horror I was instantly aware that the prayer meeting was indeed a séance. I registered my protest.

I explained to the people that the Bible takes a very dim view of such practices. I cited passages from the Old Testament where such activity was called an abomination to God and was a capital crime in the nation of Israel. The immediate reply from the leader was, "But that's the Old Testament. We live in New

Testament times now, and the Spirit has assured us that this is His will today."

I asked the following question: "What has happened in the scope of redemptive history to make God change His mind about this?" To be sure, there are certain things that were forbidden in the Old Testament that are permitted today (such as dietary restrictions). There were also things commanded in the Old Testament that would be offensive to God if we practiced them now (such as sacrificial offerings that would now do insult to the finished perfect sacrifice of Christ). With these changes in the economy of God there are clear reasons given by the Bible itself why the changes are made. But not a single word of Scripture gives the slightest hint that the practice of necromancy, which was an abomination to God in the Old Testament, is something that is now pleasing to God. On the contrary, the New Testament is as opposed to sorcery and magic as the Old Testament, as we see from the apostolic confrontation with such practices in the Book of Acts.

But we still must ask, Is spiritualism a type of magic or sorcery? Did not Saul have the witch of Endor call Samuel back from the grave?

How are we to understand this macabre incident recorded in the Old Testament? Did the witch really bring back Samuel or his ghost? Was it simply a magician's trick?

Frankly, I don't know the answer to that question. The Old Testament narrative certainly sounds like it was a genuine retrieval of Samuel from the grave:

And the king said to her, "Do not be afraid. What did you see?" And the woman said to Saul, "I saw a spirit

ascending out of the earth." So he said to her, "What is
his form?" And she said, "An old man is coming up,
and he is covered with a mantle." And Saul perceived
that it was Samuel, and he stooped with his face to the
ground and bowed down. Now Samuel said to Saul,
"Why have you disturbed me by bringing me up?"
1 Samuel 28:13-15

The narrative here may be presenting a description
of a real medium-conjured retrieval. It may also simply
be a faithful record of the phenomenon as it appeared.
The Bible frequently uses what we call *phenomeno-*
logical language, language that describes events *as they*
appear to the naked eye. This means simply that a
magician's clever trick would be described just as it
appeared to the witnesses.

For example, we might ask, Did Pharaoh's court
magicians perform real magic, or is the biblical record
of their deeds done in competition with the miracles of
Moses simply a phenomenological description of their
cleverly devised tricks?

Many scholars seek another alternative. They put
the tricks of the magicians and the witch of Endor's
feat in the category of satanic miracles. The Bible
attributes to Satan the power of performing "signs,
and lying wonders" (2 Thessalonians 2:9). That is,
Satan, disguised as an angel of light, can perform
counterfeit miracles.

Can Satan Do Miracles?

I think that it is safe to assume that the vast majority
of evangelical Christians believe that Satan has the
power to perform miracles. I do not believe that he

can. This puts me in a decided minority in the evangelical world.

The issue centers around two questions: What is the biblical function of miracles? What is a *lying* wonder? That is, what is it about a counterfeit miracle that makes it counterfeit rather than the genuine article?

Theologians make an important distinction regarding miracles that warrants our mention. Some define a miracle as an action that is performed *contra naturam*—that is, it is an action that is performed that works against the normal laws of nature. Added to this concept is the idea of a work performed *contra peccatum*—that is an action *against* sin.

Now the majority report goes like this: The Devil can perform works against nature (*contra naturam*), but he cannot perform works against sin (*contra peccatum*). This argument rests primarily upon the New Testament debate between Jesus and the Pharisees. The Pharisees did not deny that Jesus performed miracles. Rather they accused Jesus of performing His miracles by the power of Satan (Mark 3:22).

This accusation provoked Jesus to give His solemn warning against committing blasphemy against the Holy Spirit (Mark 3:28-30). Jesus responded to the charge by saying that Satan would not perform works that would undermine his own agenda. Here Jesus spoke about a house divided against itself.

So He called them to Him and said to them in parables, "How can Satan cast out Satan? If a kingdom is divided against itself, that kingdom cannot stand. And if a house is divided against itself that house cannot stand." Mark 3:23-25

We notice that Jesus did not respond to His accusers by saying, "Satan does not have the power to do real miracles." Jesus did not dispute the Devil's ability to work *contra naturam*. Rather, He indicated the folly of thinking that Satan would ever act *contra peccatum*. Therefore the conclusion is reached by many that Jesus allowed the inference that Satan can in fact perform miracles.

This would mean, then, that the crucial difference between a genuine miracle from God and a counterfeit miracle from Satan would lie in its ultimate purpose. A genuine miracle would be done to destroy the work of Satan and promote the kingdom of God, while a counterfeit miracle would be designed to undermine the Kingdom of God and promote the kingdom of Satan. Both "miracles," however, would actually defy the normal laws of nature.

This distinction is certainly tempting to embrace and has been very persuasive to many. We are still left, however, with some very thorny problems. The big problem is this: How do we ultimately know who is performing the real miracle and who the counterfeit? It is not so self-evident who is promoting the kingdom of God and who isn't.

We remember that one of Satan's undisputed powers is to masquerade as an angel of light. That is, he has the ability to appear "under the auspices of the good." Satan's masquerade is incredibly subtle. He does not announce himself as the prince of darkness. He gives all the outward appearances of light. How are we to see through the disguise and penetrate to the truth?

I am going to ask the Christian to think the unthinkable: How do we know that Jesus was not a false prophet? How do we know that Jesus Himself

was not the Devil in disguise, doing extraordinary
miracles, including His own resurrection, to seduce
people away from orthodox Judaism and Old
Testament monotheism? How do we know that
Christianity is not the great delusion sent from Satan
to get millions of people to practice idolatry by
worshiping a man or an angel rather than God
Himself?

To ask such questions, even hypothetically, is to
come precariously close to the unpardonable sin. But
the questions are legitimate. If they are not, then we
can never honestly ask, How do we know that Jesus is
the Christ?

Let us use a hypothetical argument. Imagine that
Satan did masquerade as a false messiah and that he
did all kinds of miracles to support the awful
deception. Then suppose that some godly Pharisees
noticed that this false messiah was promoting worship
of Himself and was undermining their understanding
of the law of Moses and they confronted this false
messiah with the charge that he was in a league with the
Devil. What would the false messiah say? He would
certainly not declare that He was working for sin. He
might be subtle enough to confuse his opponents by
saying that Satan wouldn't work against Satan. True
enough but Satan is surely clever enough to get people
to think he is working against himself while all the
time He is actually working for himself.

In other words, how would we know if Satan were
in fact working against himself? When Jesus used this
argument against the Pharisees the argument was not
standing alone in isolation from a host of other
assumptions that were already shared by the Pharisees.
For example, Jesus repeatedly appealed to the

Scriptures to support His claims to Messiahship.

But Satan also appealed to Scripture. Two prior questions must be solved before the *contra peccatum* argument can have any validity. The two questions are these: How do we know the Scriptures are the Word of God? Who is interpreting the Scriptures correctly?

The second question is not always easy to answer, but we do have certain rules of interpretation (hermeneutics) that go a long way to help us. The big question is the first question: How do we know that the Scriptures are the Word of God?

If we can first establish that the Scriptures are the Word of God and then show that Satan's interpretation of Scripture is invalid, *then* we could know that Satan is working against God. Before we can ever establish that a word or a deed is performed *contra peccatum* or *pro peccatum* we must first establish the nature of the *peccatum*. That is, before we can ever know that something is working against the norms of God we must first establish what those norms are. This is precisely what Scripture does.

Only God can prove that His word is indeed His word. How does He do that? He does it by miracles. He does it by performing works *contra naturam*. God shows that something comes from Him by attesting to it with works that only God can do. If God attests something by doing a work that Satan can do as well, then all that is proven is that the work proceeds from *either* God or Satan. If that were the case we would have no possible way of knowing which of the two were in fact the author of the work.

Moses had an experience with a bush that was burning but not being consumed. He had a firsthand encounter with an activity that was *contra naturam*. In

the burning bush episode God commanded Moses to
lead the children of Israel out of the captivity they
suffered under. Moses was understandably concerned
about his own lack of credentials. He had been in
obscure exile for decades. Who would believe his claim
to be acting under divine directives? He said to God,

*"Suppose they will not believe me or listen to my
voice; suppose they say, 'The LORD has not appeared
to you.'" So the LORD said to him, "What is that in
your hand?" And he said, "A rod." And He said, "Cast
it on the ground." So he cast it on the ground, and it
became a serpent; and Moses fled from it.*
Exodus 4:1-3

God furnished credentials for Moses by giving him
the power to perform miracles. The miracles would
prove that Moses had the authority of God behind him

*that they may believe that the LORD God of their
fathers, the God of Abraham, the God of Isaac, and
the God of Jacob, has appeared to you.* Exodus 4:5

The Fakery of Magicians

When Moses and Aaron arrived at the court of
Pharaoh, they were soon engaged in a contest of
"miracles" with the magicians of Egypt. Moses had
Aaron throw down his staff and it turned into a snake.
The Egyptian magicians then duplicated the feat. They
threw down their staffs and they turned into snakes as
well (Exodus 7:10-12).

What are we to make of this? Were Pharaoh's
magicians empowered by Satan to perform bona fide

miracles? Was this a contest between one man who was working *contra peccatum* and a group of men who were working *pro peccatum*? How would any bystander be able to discern the difference?

The contest was settled on *natural* grounds, not *moral* grounds. Moses won because his snake ate up the snakes of the magicians. In subsequent contests Moses won every time on the sheer strength of his superiority of power. On each occasion the magicians reached a limit beyond which they could not go. Moses was able to break through the limits of the magicians.

It is important to note that the Bible calls the magicians of Pharaoh "magicians." They were not demons. They were human beings practicing the esoteric art of Egyptian magic.

The question remains: Were the Egyptian magicians wielding supernatural power, or were they simply practicing the accomplished tricks of their trade by quite natural means?

There is no reason to assume that the magicians of Pharaoh could do anything more astonishing than contemporary American magicians can perform. Modern-day magicians such as Doug Henning and David Copperfield do not claim to be doing real "magic." They prefer to call themselves professional illusionists. Through cleverly devised tricks and/or sleight of hand they can perform feats that leave their audiences astounded. Yet they perform these tricks in a culture that, for the most part, is not inclined to believe that magicians have supernatural powers.

I once visited the Magic Palace in Los Angeles. The Palace is a delightful dinner club reserved for professional magicians and their guests. To be a member a magician must pass an entrance test judged by their peers. As meals are served visiting magicians display their tricks for the guests. On my visit to the palace I was treated to a one-hour show by the world's best sleight of hand artist. The show took place at our table. The magician sat two feet away from me. He placed three saltshakers on the table and placed a twenty-five cent piece under one of the saltshakers. Before my eyes he moved the saltshakers around until suddenly the quarter disappeared. Then it would turn up under a different saltshaker. I watched him do this for an hour, trying as hard as I could to catch him changing positions. I never caught him. I tried different techniques. For example, I stared steadfastly at shaker Number 3, refusing to look away from it no matter what the magician did. He went through his routine and then asked me, "Is it under Number 3?" I said, "No!" He replied, "Too late!" and lifted 3 to reveal the quarter underneath it.

I still don't know how he did it. But I knew it wasn't by supernatural power.

Most magicians' tricks are done by quite simple means. Often the most astonishing tricks are done by the simplest means. Use is made of mirrors, collapsible boxes, hinges, or simple sleight of hand. Usually the magician depends upon an assumption that he gets the audience to make, which is an erroneous assumption.

I like to do simple card tricks. Some of them are done via mathematics, others require a measure of physical dexterity. The easiest are the ones performed by depending on erroneous assumptions.

Before he died, Jackie Gleason related a story of a modern-day wizard. Gleason was lured into a conversation about mental telepathy by comic Lou

Costello in Miami. Costello insisted that there were people who could perform amazing telepathic feats. He said that he knew of a man who could read people's minds over the telephone. Gleason was aghast at Costello's apparent credulity and declared that mental telepathy was bunk. As the debate continued Costello stood his ground and finally offered to bet Gleason five hundred dollars that he could prove his point. Gleason accepted the bet and the scam was on.

Costello produced a deck of cards and asked Gleason to pick a card from the deck. Gleason picked a card (say the Queen of Spades). Then Costello said, "OK, here's the Wizard's phone number in Boston. Call this number and ask for the Wizard." Gleason dialed the number and said, "May I speak to the Wizard?" The voice in Boston replied, "This is the Wizard." Gleason said, "I've just picked a card out of a deck, and I want you to tell me the card." The voice replied, "First you must concentrate intensely on the card."

Gleason stood at the phone thinking for all he was worth about the Queen of Spades. The Wizard hesitated and then said, "Your card is a picture card. It's a black card. You selected the Queen of Spades."

Gleason dropped the phone in shock and turned to the grinning Costello who was standing with his palm out to receive five hundred dollars.

Lou Costello made a lot of money out of his "Wizard" scam. His game was simple. He had fifty-two friends scattered across the country. Each friend was a designated wizard of a specific card. Costello memorized the phone number of each friend corresponding to each card in the deck of cards. Then he would lure pigeons like Jackie Gleason into discussions about mental telepathy. He had people pleading with him to make a bet about proving his point. Once his victim selected a card, all Costello had to do was give the appropriate telephone number and instruct the victim to call and ask for the Wizard. Anytime a designated Wizard received a telephone call requesting a wizard he knew Costello's scam was on and that he could expect a cut of the winnings.

What does all this have to do with the witch of Endor and Pharaoh's magicians? The point is this: The court magicians of Egypt and the witch of Endor were in all probability simply practicing clever tricks that were designed to amaze their audiences. It is no great feat to conceal a snake in a collapsible tube. It requires little more planning than a TV magician who saws a lady in half or produces a rabbit out of an apparently empty hat. The difference between God's miracle with Moses and that of the Egyptian magicians is that God turned Moses' rod into a snake, not a rod He prepared beforehand and brought to the occasion.

What about Saul and the Witch of Endor?

The witch of Endor presents more difficulty. We can explain it in several possible ways. The first is that it was a trick done in a similar manner performed by modern mediums. The second is that it was a demonic illusion performed by satanic means. The third is that Samuel was in fact brought back from the dead.

If the third alternative actually took place, then we do have a biblical record of a ghost appearing from the other side. However, this would not endorse the practice of séances. Even in this episode the witch of Endor was guilty of practicing something that, fraudulent or real, was still a capital offense in Israel. She was well aware of that.

Then the woman said to him, "Look, you know what Saul has done, how he has cut off the mediums and the spiritists from the land, why then do you lay a snare for my life to cause me to die?" And Saul swore to her by the LORD saying, "As the LORD lives, no punishment shall come upon you for this thing."
1 Samuel 28:9-10

If it is possible to contact the dead, it is not permissible. That much we know for sure. Consider just a few of the biblical prohibitions against it:

You shall not permit a sorceress to live. Exodus 22:18

Give no regard to mediums and familiar spirits; do not seek after them to be defiled by them; I am the LORD your God. Leviticus 19:31

And the person who turns after mediums and familiar spirits, to prostitute himself with them, I will set my face against that person and cut him off from his people. Leviticus 20:6

A man or a woman who is a medium, or who has familiar spirits, shall surely be put to death; they shall stone them with stones. Their blood shall be upon them. Leviticus 20:27

In the last chapter of the New Testament sorcerers are included among those who are excluded from heaven.

*But outside are dogs and sorcerers and sexually
immoral and murderers and idolaters, and whoever
loves and practices a lie.* Revelation 22:15

Exposing the Fakery

Contemporary spiritists and mediums are adroit at
practicing a lie. Along the city streets of America we
see signs advertising palm readers who promise to tell
us our futures for a fee. The crystal ball trade gives
little outward appearance of prosperity. Most of these
establishments are located in run-down sections of
towns where the palmists prey on the poor, promising
them hope for the future. One wonders why these
fortune-tellers don't concentrate their psychic energy,
tarot cards, and the like on the stock market and retire
as wealthy investors in six months.

I once knew a man who earned a Ph.D. from
Harvard University in one of the natural sciences. The
man was a Christian and an amateur magician. He
used to go to churches and lecture on the fraudulent
means used by modern mediums in their séances. He
duplicated their feats on stage and then exposed them.
One routine he performed went like this:

The scientist got a group of people from the
audience to come on stage and sit around a table.
They all held hands, making sure the scientist's hands
were firmly in the grasp of others. Then he instructed
the participants to put their feet on his shoes. While
the audience watched, he announced that he would
call on a departed spirit to indicate its presence by
rapping on the table. The man was wearing specially
weighted shoes with steel toes. He had a piece of metal
taped under his trousers at his knee. While the
participants pressed down on his toes under the table,

he simply slipped his feet out of his shoes and lifted his knee and began rapping the metal against the underside of the table. While those seated around the table looked in astonishment, the people in the audience who could see what he was doing were roaring in laughter.

Sir Arthur Conan Doyle, the author of the famous Sherlock Holmes series, was deeply involved in a society that was devoted to medium practices. Sir Arthur was convinced in the authenticity of the practice. The spiritualists' greatest enemy of the day was the noted illusionist, Harry Houdini. Houdini was convinced that all noted spiritualism was based on fraud. He offered a lucrative reward to any medium who could perform any feat that Houdini could not duplicate by natural trickery. No one ever collected the reward.

Houdini went even further. Before he died he arranged a date and a set of signals by which, if it were possible, he would contact his wife after he died. On the appointed date after his death, the great Houdini was not able to make the prearranged contact. Even posthumously Houdini discredited the trade of the mediums.

It takes a thief to catch a thief. Mediums that have impressed scientific investigators have been exposed by professional magicians. Magicians tend to be the best ghostbusters of all. They know the carefully guarded secrets of the tricksters.

Going Beyond the Occult to the Truth

If we desire confirmation for life after death there is a better place to look for it than in the realm of magic or

the occult. We can go beyond the speculation of
philosophers, the mumbo-jumbo of the occultists, and
the legerdemain of the illusionists. We go to the New
Testament, to the words and work of Jesus that
transcend the fraudulent and bring us into the realm of
sober, historical truth.

The miracles performed by Jesus were not designed
to prove the existence of God. Miracles do not prove
the existence of God because miracles cannot prove
the existence of God. Why not? For a miracle to be
recognized as a miracle it must first be established that
God exists. A miracle may be defined as being an
action that only the power of God can perform.

In the Bible the function of miracle is not to prove
the existence of God but to prove the endorsement of
God. Miracles are appealed to by the biblical writers
as "signs." These signs "signify" the stamp of God's
approval. They are means of divine authentication of
God's messengers, His designated agents of
supernatural revelation. The author of Hebrews gives
this testimony:

*How shall we escape if we neglect so great a salvation,
which at the first began to be spoken by the Lord, and
was confirmed to us by those who heard Him, God
also bearing witness both with signs and wonders,
with various miracles, and gifts of the Holy Spirit,
according to His own will?* Hebrews 2:3-4

Nicodemus was thinking soundly when he
approached Jesus at night and said, "Rabbi, we know
that You are a teacher come from God; for no one can
do these signs that You do unless God is with him"
(John 3:2).

Nicodemus understood that miracles are a divine accreditation. Just as God endorsed Moses and Elijah (the Law and the Prophets) by miracles, so He also certified Jesus and the apostles by the same means.

Now suppose, as indeed many Christians do, that Satan can also perform real miracles. What would the implications be? In a word, they would be catastrophic to the Christian faith. As I said earlier, if Satan can perform real miracles then the Bible's appeal to miracles, as well as Jesus' appeal to His works as a credential, would be invalid. Since we would first have to establish the norm of God's revelation to evaluate who is performing miracles for or against sin (*pro* or *contra peccatum*), the appeal to scriptural norms to settle such a debate would be the worst case of reasoning in a vicious circle. The argument is a classical example of the fallacy of "begging the question."

Why is this so? If someone besides God can supply the power for a miracle then obviously the sheer presence of a miracle could never prove divine attestation. As I formerly labored the point, the most such a miracle could indicate would be that either God or Satan was being represented. Without a norm to discern between these two miracles we would have no validating power for agents of revelation.

We conclude that when the Bible describes the "miracles" of Satan as lying signs and wonders, the accent is on the qualifying adjective *lying*. It is not that Satan performs real miracles to support a lie but rather that the miracles themselves are fraudulent. The lie is found in this: the apparent miracle is not really a miracle at all, it is a cleverly devised trick, more clever than any human can perform. But these tricks always reach a limit—a limit bounded by the laws of nature themselves. Satan cannot bring life out of death or create something out of nothing. The power to create and the keys of life and death belong to God and to His Christ. These powers are not granted to the enemy. Satan may be able to out-Houdini Houdini, but he cannot out perform the Christ. He and his works are bathed in the lie. They have no part in what is authentic.

The problem becomes even more complicated when we ask if modern-day healers can do bona fide miracles.

Toward a Definition of Miracle

How we answer this question will depend in large measure upon how we define a miracle. The popular definition is that any supernatural or even natural event that ultimately proceeds from God can be called a "miracle." The word *miracle* is used rather loosely by people, especially by evangelical Christians.

We often hear people describe the beauty of a sunset or the birth of a baby as a miracle. Indeed, sunsets and babies are marvelous manifestations of God's creation and providence. But strictly speaking they are not miracles. The birth of a baby is both ordinary and natural. There is nothing *contra naturam* about human birth (unless the baby is born of a virgin). To be sure, the laws that govern natural human procreation are God's laws. All of nature ultimately depends upon supernature both for its origin and its sustenance. But natural laws describe the ordinary course of God's government of this world. It is precisely this ordinary course of nature that makes it possible for the extraordinary significance of a real miracle.

We must add the further distinction, all miracles are supernatural events, but not all supernatural events are miracles. For example, the regeneration of a human soul by the immediate influence of the Holy Spirit is a supernatural event. It is an action that only God can perform. Luther was content to call it a miracle precisely because of its immediate supernatural character. I would hesitate to call it a miracle because I prefer a tighter definition of a miracle.

Theologians have provided a tight, technical definition of a miracle: A miracle is an extraordinary work in the external perceivable world that is wrought by the immediate supernatural power of God, that is *contra naturam*. It is a work that only the power of God can perform such as bringing life out of death or something out of nothing. We see at once that theologians who use this definition of a miracle get in hot water with lay persons who speak of miracles in more general terms. I cringe, for example, when someone asks me if miracles happen today. I don't like to answer the question because the matter is so complex that it is inevitable that when I say no, people will think that I am denying that God is working supernaturally today.

Before I continue let me say this. I firmly believe in the authenticity of biblical miracles. I firmly believe that God is working today and working supernaturally today. He is answering prayers. He is healing people who are sick, even by extraordinary providence. But having said all this, I must add: I do not think that anyone is doing miracles today according to the tight technical definition I have offered.

Are There Miracles Today?

Why do I put a limit here? Someone will inevitably ask, Aren't you limiting God? I answer, By no means. The question is not, *Can* God do miracles today? Obviously, if God is God He can perform miracles anywhere and anytime He desires. The question is, *Is* God doing miracles today?

I think God is not performing miracles, in the narrow sense, today. The reason I think that is because I am convinced that there are no agents of normative revelation around today. That is, there are no Apostles (with a capital *A*) alive today.

To get this crucial point we must think closely and carefully. The biblical prophets and apostles were agents of normative supernatural revelation. They appealed to miracles as God's certification that they were *bona fide* agents of revelation. Now suppose God gave the power of miracles to people who were not agents of revelation. If both agents of revelation and non-agents of revelation could perform miracles, then surely the sheer presence of miracle-working power could not serve as proof that a person was an agent of revelation. How could it possibly certify an agent of revelation if a non-agent of revelation could do the same thing? It is not the claims of faith-healers that I'm concerned about here. It is the claims of Jesus, Moses, and the Apostle Paul we're concerned about. We simply cannot have our theological cake and eat it too.

Oral Roberts has claimed that he raised people from the dead in his ministry. When pressured by the news media he fudged a bit on these claims. It is one thing for people to be revived through CPR or other forms of resuscitation. That happens with ever-increasing frequency. It is quite another for a person to be decomposing in the grave for several days and be brought back to life as Lazarus was by the divine command of Jesus.

It is noteworthy that the famous miracle-workers of our day do not perform their feats at cemeteries.

There are also people who claim to be recipients of special divine revelation today. One well-known speaker even published the text of a divine revelation he received about the future of south Florida. These people claim to be agents of *normative* revelation. Again the question is begged. If the text of the speaker's prophecy was indeed the supernaturally inspired Word of God, why shouldn't its content appear in a new revised edition of the New Testament? Surely this speaker would shrink in horror at such a suggestion, but my question is, Why? If he's receiving the very Word of God that will affect every resident of south Florida, I would think he wouldn't rest until that message was published as widely as the Bible, indeed, as part of the Bible itself. The man is claiming no less authority than the Bible claims, and no less relevance for its message.

I'm afraid that the real reason people do not press to have their private prophecies published in the New Testament is because they know very well that such a request would instantly discredit them among their followers.

Great Resources for Christian Living— from R. C. Sproul

CHOSEN BY GOD   0-8423-1335-4
Gain insight into the doctrine of predestination through this clear, biblical presentation.

ESSENTIAL TRUTHS OF THE CHRISTIAN FAITH
0-8423-5936-2
Categorized for easy reference, more than 100 doctrines offer a basic understanding of Christianity.

FOLLOWING CHRIST   0-8423-5937-0
This combination of four power-packed books will challenge you to become a mature follower of Jesus Christ.

THE GLORY OF CHRIST   0-8423-1617-5
This intriguing focus on the life, person, and deity of Christ is third in Sproul's trilogy on the Trinity.

THE HOLINESS OF GOD   0-8423-1365-6
A best-selling treatment of what is perhaps God's least understood dimension is developed in this first volume in Sproul's trilogy on the Trinity.

IF THERE'S A GOD, WHY ARE THERE ATHEISTS?
0-8423-1565-9
Here is excellent guidance for Christians who have doubts or who want to respond intelligently to skeptics.

THE INTIMATE MARRIAGE   0-8423-1610-8
Develop marriage skills that will lead you past potential problems into joyous communion with your spouse.

THE MYSTERY OF THE HOLY SPIRIT   0-8423-4378-4
Second in Sproul's trilogy on the Trinity, this book covers the role and nature of the Holy Spirit.

PLEASING GOD   0-8423-5024-1
The author shows how God delights in those who seek after righteousness.

THE SOUL'S QUEST FOR GOD   0-8423-6088-3
Find deeper intimacy with God through obedience to him and the power of the Holy Spirit.

SURPRISED BY SUFFERING   0-8423-6624-5
With concern for biblical truth, Sproul addresses the afterlife and the role of suffering in human experience.